HOW TO MAKE 100

Bead Embroidery Motifs

Creative Publishing international

First published in the United States of America by Creative Publishing international, Inc., a member of Quayside Publishing Group
400 First Avenue North
Suite 400
Minneapolis, MN 55401

1-800-328-3895
www.creativepub.com

Visit www.Craftside.Typepad.com for a behind-the-scenes peek at our crafty world!

ISBN: 978-1-58923-779-7
10 9 8 7 6 5 4 3 2 1
Digital edition published in 2014
eISBN: 978-1-61058-892-8

Library of Congress Cataloging-in-Publication Data available

Copy Editor: Kari Cornell
Proofreader: Karen Ruth
Cover Design: Creative Publishing International, Inc.
Page Layout: barefoot art graphic design
Illustrations: Clifford Crabe
Photographs: Lightstream Photography

Printed in China

HOW TO MAKE 100

Bead Embroidery Motifs

Inspiration and Instructions for Plant, Animal, Abstract, and Icon Designs

GENEVIÈVE CRABE

Creative Publishing
international

Contents

Introduction

I became interested in bead embroidery in 2007 and joined Robin Atkins' Bead Journal Project (BJP). All participants were asked to create twelve pieces of bead embroidery over the course of a year. Through my work on the project, I learned a tremendous amount about designing and stitching bead embroidery pieces. When I was searching for a theme for my pages, I came across my late mother's sketchbooks. My mother, Suzanne La Palme, spent her career as an embroidery designer in the garment district in Montréal. Her sketchbooks are filled with ideas that she used in her work, and I chose twelve of her sketches for my BJP pieces. A few of the motifs in this book are also inspired by her sketches.

Bead Journal Project

Today, bead embroidery remains my favorite kind of beadwork. I have designed the motifs in this book to exercise a variety of techniques and use a wide assortment of beads and embellishments, but I encourage you to substitute from your own stash.

The motifs also can be used to embellish garments, quilts, or accessories like bags or purses.

I use motifs to make jewelry, especially brooches like these.

If you are new to bead embroidery, begin with Techniques (page 120), which contains photos and diagrams explaining all the stitches used in the motifs. Even if you have some experience, I encourage you to review the Techniques, because the names of stitches are not standard. Refer to Supplies (page 118) if you have any questions about a particular item. I've also included a Resources and Suppliers list (page 127).

The motifs are divided into chapters according to theme. Each motif page includes four parts: an enlarged photo of the finished motif, an actual-size line diagram, an Ingredients list, and the written instructions, which I call the Recipe. The Ingredients lists specify the type and color of beads. On some pages there may also be a tip that can help in your execution of the design. Note that the diagram is the actual size of the finished motif, so you can trace and transfer the outline directly to your fabric. For details on how to transfer the design, see page 125. The numbers on the diagram correspond to the steps in the Recipe.

- Recipe
- Finished motif
- Actual-size line diagram
- Ingredients
- Tips

Recipe

Actual-size line diagram

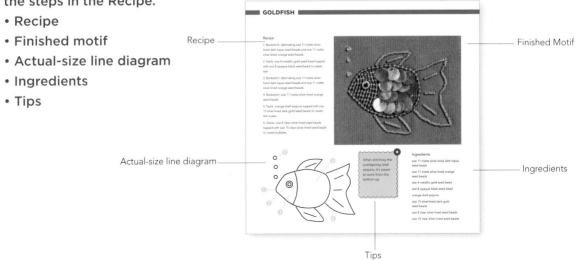

Finished Motif

Ingredients

Tips

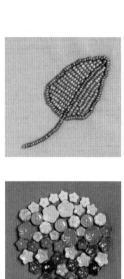

Flora and Fauna

This chapter includes a collection of floral motifs, as well as some butterfly, bird, and fish motifs. These designs are commonly used in both traditional thread embroidery and bead embroidery. The first few motifs are simple designs that provide a great introduction to this technique.

SIMPLE LEAF

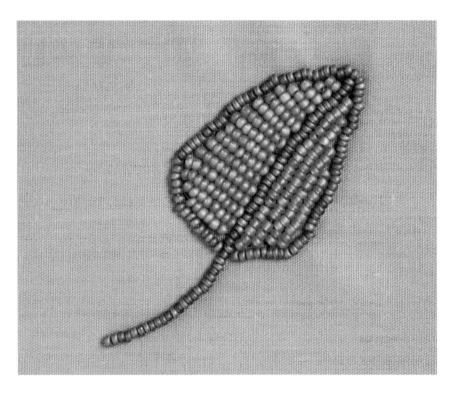

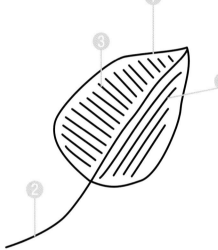

Ingredients

size 10 matte opaque green AB seed beads

size 10 matte opaque light green AB seed beads

Recipe

1, 2. Backstitch: size 10 matte opaque green AB seed beads to outline the leaf and make the vein and stem.

3. Backstitch: size 10 matte opaque light green AB seed beads in lines to fill left side of leaf.

4. Backstitch: size 10 matte opaque light green AB seed beads in lines to fill right side of leaf.

Add dimension to the design by laying out the lines in two different directions. This causes the light to reflect differently on the two sides of the leaf.

Recipe

1. Stack: two felt flowers topped with a size 8 metallic gold seed bead and a size 11 metallic gold seed bead.

2. Single bead stitch: metal butterfly bead with a size 8 opaque black seed bead on each side.

3. Running stitch: black embroidery floss to create butterfly's trail.

Ingredients

four felt flowers

two size 8 metallic gold seed beads

two size 11 metallic gold seed beads

metal butterfly bead

two size 8 opaque black seed beads

black embroidery floss

GRAPES

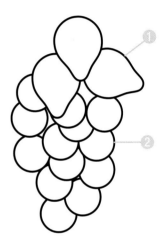

Ingredients

pressed glass light and dark green leaf beads

size 15 clear seed beads

red dyed shell sequins

Recipe

1. Stacks: pressed glass light and dark green leaf beads, topped with size 15 clear seed beads.

2. Stacks: red dyed shell sequins topped with size 15 clear seed beads.

To give dimension to your design, overlap the shapes.

Recipe

1. Backstitch: size 10 matte blue AB seed beads to create flower.

2. Backstitch: size 10 matte light green AB seed beads to form leaves.

3. Loops: size 11 opaque yellow seed beads to make flower center.

To achieve the same look more quickly, use couching here instead of backstitch.

Ingredients

size 10 matte blue AB seed beads

size 10 matte light green AB seed beads

size 11 opaque yellow seed beads

BRIGHT EYES

Ingredients

die-cut felt flower

fabric glue

polymer clay face

size 10 metallic gold seed beads

Recipe

1. Glue die-cut felt flower to fabric.

2. Glue polymer clay face to center of felt flower.

3. Scatter stitch: size 10 metallic gold seed beads on the flower petals.

When attaching the felt flower to the background fabric, apply glue only to the center of the felt piece. Then when stitching the beads, you won't have to push your needle through dried glue. The stitches used to apply the seed beads will hold down the petals.

FIVE-PETAL WITH LEAVES

Recipe

1. Single bead stitch: black and copper glass leaves to create flower.

2. Loops: size 10 silver-lined topaz seed beads to form flower center.

3. Backstitch: size 11 green mix seed beads to make leaves.

When adding a leaf bead, insert your needle through the fabric and the bead several times so that the leaf will remain in the correct orientation.

Ingredients

black and copper glass leaves

size 10 silver-lined topaz seed beads

size 11 green mix seed beads

RAINBOW BOUQUET

Recipe

1. Stack stitch: a variety of glass flower beads in yellow, orange, and red, all topped with size 15 gold silver-lined seed beads to create the left side of the flower.

2. Stack stitch: a variety of glass flower beads in blue and turquoise, all topped with size 15 clear silver-lined seed beads to create the right side of the flower.

Ingredients

variety of glass flower beads in yellow, orange, and red

size 15 gold silver-lined seed beads

variety of glass flower beads in blue and turquoise

size 15 clear silver-lined seed beads

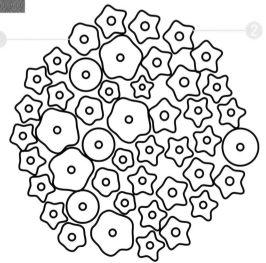

DOGWOOD

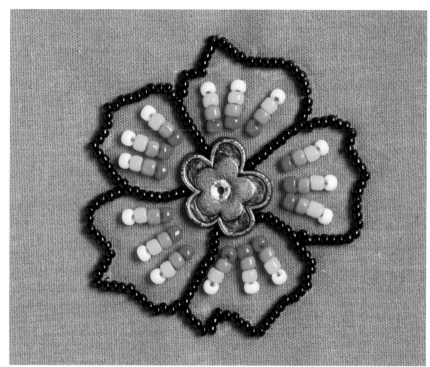

Recipe

1. Glue flat-back metal flower scrapbooking embellishment to fabric.

2. Glue small clear flat-back crystal to metal flower.

3. Backstitch: size 11 opaque black seed beads to form outer edge of petals.

4. Backstitch: size 8 opaque white, yellow, orange, and red seed beads in lines from center of petals.

Ingredients

flat-back metal flower scrapbooking embellishment

fabric glue

small clear flat-back crystal

size 11 opaque black seed beads

size 8 opaque white, yellow, orange, and red seed beads

BEADED LACE ROSE

Ingredients

lace flower

size 11 green-lined light topaz seed beads

size 10 metallic gold seed beads

Recipe

1. Place lace flower on fabric.

2. Backstitch: size 11 green-lined light topaz seed beads to create edges of leaves.

3. Backstitch: size 10 metallic gold seed beads to form petals.

4. Scatter stitch: size 10 metallic gold seed beads to color flower center.

FELT ECHOES

Placing the darker felt leaf under and slightly offset from the lighter leaf gives the illusion of a shadow.

Recipe

1. Layer two felt leaves, slightly offset.

2. Layer two pink felt flowers above leaves.

3. Stack on top of the felt flowers, in center: a yellow flower glass bead topped with a size 11 green-lined light topaz seed bead.

4. Backstitch: size 11 green-lined light topaz seed beads to define leaves.

Ingredients

two felt leaves

two pink felt flowers

yellow flower glass bead

size 11 green-lined light topaz seed beads

Recipe

1. Stack four felt flowers, with largest on bottom and smallest on top.

2. Individual stitches from the center to the edge of flower with metallic gold embroidery thread.

3. Stack stitch: a round gold-tone spacer bead topped with a size 6 opaque black seed bead.

4. Backstitch: metallic gold bugles and size 11 metallic gold seed beads.

Ingredients

four felt flowers, same shape but different sizes

metallic gold embroidery thread

round gold-tone spacer bead

size 6 opaque black seed bead

metallic gold bugles

size 11 metallic gold seed beads

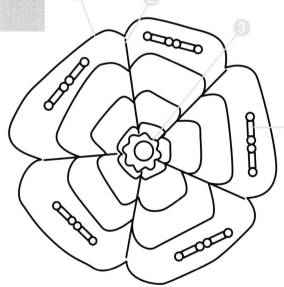

Recipe

1. Stack: felt leaves and felt flowers, topped with a size 8 metallic gold seed bead and a size 11 metallic gold seed bead to form flowers.

2. Backstitch: size 11 opaque green frosted AB seed beads to create flower stems.

3. Glue dragonfly charm to fabric.

Ingredients

six felt leaves

three felt flowers

size 8 metallic gold seed bead

size 11 metallic gold seed bead

size 11 opaque green frosted AB seed beads

dragonfly charm

fabric glue

BERRY BRANCH

Ingredients

size 11 green-lined transparent light topaz seed beads

red sequins

size 10 metallic gold seed beads

Recipe

1. Backstitch: size 11 green-lined transparent light topaz seed beads to create flower stems.

2. Small leaves: size 11 green-lined transparent light topaz seed beads to outline leaves.

3. Stack: red sequins topped with size 10 metallic gold seed beads to create flowers.

MUSHROOM

Recipe

1. Backstitch: size 8 matte silver-lined red seed beads to create mushroom top.

2. Backstitch: size 11 matte silver-lined dark topaz seed beads to create mushroom stem.

3. Backstitch: size 11 matte silver-lined dark topaz seed beads to form lines on stem.

4. Backstitch: size 8 matte silver-lined red seed beads to form lines on mushroom top.

5. Scatter stitch: size 11 opaque white seed beads to decorate mushroom top.

Ingredients

size 8 matte silver-lined red seed beads

size 11 matte silver-lined dark topaz seed beads

size 8 matte silver-lined red seed beads

size 11 opaque white seed beads

Ingredients

dark green rattail cord

green thread

six felt flowers in two sizes

three yellow glass flower beads

three size 11 opaque black seed beads

size 10 dark red AB seed beads

Recipe

1. Couch: dark green rattail cord with green thread to create flower stems.

2. Stacks: two felt flowers and a yellow glass flower bead, topped with a size 11 opaque black seed bead to create flowers.

3. Backstitch and loops (over the cord): size 10 dark red AB seed beads to form tie around flower stems.

ICELANDIC POPPY

Contributed by Roxann Blazetich-Ozols

Recipe

1. Three stacks: small silver spacers topped with 3.4mm transparent yellow drops to create center of poppy.

2. Backstitch: from the center out, size 11 purple and pink cylinder beads and size 15 coral charlottes to form flower petals.

3. Backstitch: size 15 clear and matte green seed beads to create leaves.

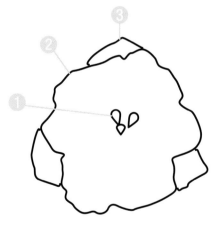

Ingredients

three small silver spacers

three 3.4mm transparent yellow drops

size 11 purple and pink cylinder beads

size 15 coral charlottes

size 15 clear and matte green seed beads

LEAF THREESOME

Ingredients

light-green felt leaf

size 11 green mix seed beads

dark-green felt leaf

medium-green felt leaf

Recipe

1. Backstitch veins: size 11 green mix seed beads on light-green felt leaf.

2. Backstitch veins: size 11 green mix seed beads on dark-green felt leaf.

3. Backstitch veins: size 11 green mix seed beads on medium-green felt leaf.

MS MUM

Recipe

1. Backstitch: size 11 red mix seed beads on orange felt flower.

2. Stack: four size 10 metallic gold seed beads in each of three stacks to create the center.

In step 1, begin stitching the beads at the tips of the petals and move towards the center.

Ingredients

orange felt flower

size 11 red mix seed beads

twelve size 10 metallic gold seed beads

SHADE TREE

Contributed by Denise Smeaton

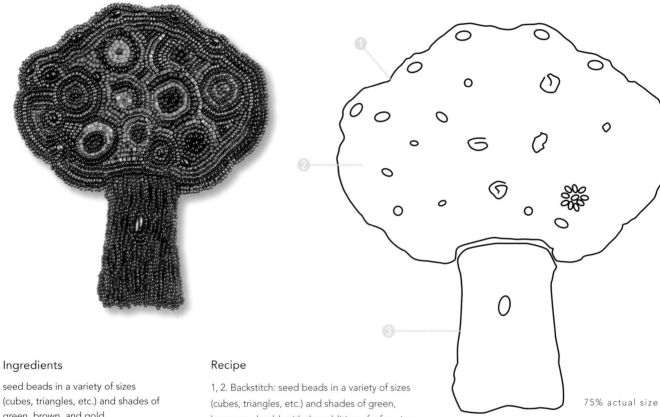

75% actual size

Ingredients

seed beads in a variety of sizes (cubes, triangles, etc.) and shades of green, brown, and gold

a few rice pearls

brown and copper seed beads

Recipe

1, 2. Backstitch: seed beads in a variety of sizes (cubes, triangles, etc.) and shades of green, brown, and gold, with the addition of a few rice pearls to create tree top.

3. Shallow loops: brown and copper seed beads, with a single rice bead to form tree trunk.

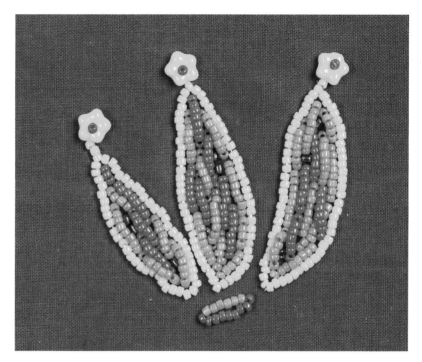

Recipe

1. Backstitch: size 8 opaque yellow seed beads to create edges of petals.

2. Mixed loops: size 11 opaque red and opaque orange seed beads to fill in petals. Use a few size 11 red silver-lined beads to fill the holes and add sparkle.

3. Leaf stitch: size 11 opaque red and opaque orange seed beads.

4. Stack: yellow flowers topped with size 11 opaque red seed beads to create flourish at top of petals.

Ingredients

size 8 opaque yellow seed beads

size 11 opaque red and opaque orange seed beads

a few size 11 red silver-lined beads

three yellow glass flower beads

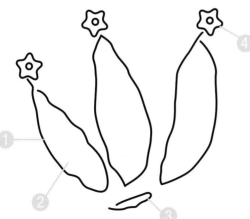

JACOBEAN FLOURISH

Contributed by Susan Sorrell

Recipe

1. Backstitch: alternating size 11 dark green and light green seed beads to create flower stems.

2. Backstitch: size 11 transparent fuchsia pink seed beads to form flower.

3. Stacks: purple button with light blue bugle topped with size 11 orange seed beads to create flower center.

4. Stitched individually: size 11 pink and orange seed beads.

5. Stack: blue size 8 bead topped with size 11 seed bead to create flower center.

6. Stitched individually: size 11 orange seeds beads.

7. Backstitch: bugles and size 11 purple seed beads.

Ingredients

size 11 dark green and light green seed beads

size 11 transparent fuchsia pink seed beads

purple button

light blue bugles

size 11 orange seed beads

size 11 pink seed beads

size 8 blue seed bead

size 11 purple seed beads

BEADED LACE BUTTERFLY

When selecting beads, try to match their shape to the shapes of the openings in the lace piece.

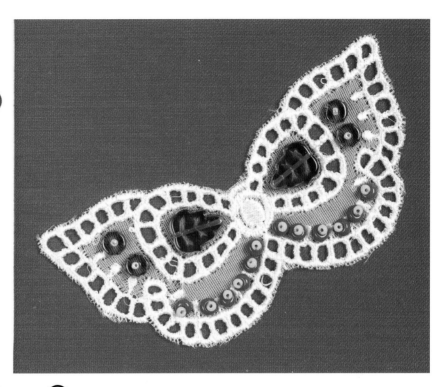

Recipe

1. Place lace butterfly on fabric.

2. Transparent blue glass leaves.

3. Stacks: transparent blue round faceted beads topped with size 15 clear seed beads.

4. Stacks: size 6 opaque red seed beads topped with size 11 opaque yellow seed beads.

Ingredients

lace butterfly

transparent blue glass leaves

transparent blue round faceted beads

size 15 clear seed beads

size 6 opaque red seed beads

size 11 opaque yellow seed beads

FELT BUTTERFLY

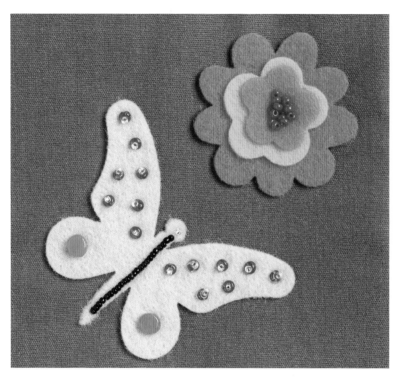

Ingredients

felt butterfly

felt flowers in three sizes

size 11 opaque red seed beads

size 15 opaque black seed beads

size 8 blue silver-lined seed beads

size 15 clear silver-lined seed beads

two 5mm flat round orange glass beads

Recipe

1. Place felt butterfly shape on fabric.

2. Stack three felt flower shapes with largest flower on bottom and smallest flower on top.

3. Loops: size 11 opaque red seed beads to form flower petals.

4. Backstitch: size 15 opaque black seed beads to make line along butterfly's body.

5. Stack stitch: size 8 blue silver-lined seed beads topped with size 15 clear silver-lined seed beads to embellish butterfly's wings.

6. Single bead stitch: 5mm flat round orange glass beads to embellish butterfly's wings.

TWEET

Recipe

1. Running stitch with light purple embroidery thread along edge of felt bird.

2. Stack: a flat orange glass bead topped with size 8 opaque black seed bead to create eye.

3. Loops: size 11 purple mix seed beads to form bird's wing.

Make the loops long and loose so they will hang down and look like feathers.

Ingredients

felt bird shape

light purple embroidery thread

a flat orange glass bead

size 8 opaque black seed bead

size 11 purple mix seed beads

HOOT

This design is based on an owl drawing by Cindy Angiel. Used with permission.

Ingredients

size 8 opaque black seed beads

two yellow, white, and black eye beads

fabric glue

yellow leaf bead

size 15 opaque black seed bead

size 11 opaque black seed beads

size 11 brown mix seed beads

size 15 opaque black seed beads

Recipe

1. Backstitch: size 8 opaque black seed beads to create bird outline.

2. Two yellow, white, and black eye beads, glued to fabric for eyes.

3. Stack: yellow leaf bead topped with size 15 opaque black seed bead to make the beak.

4. Backstitch: size 11 opaque black seed beads.

5. Shallow loops: size 11 brown mix seed beads to form feathers.

6. Backstitch: size 15 opaque black seed beads to make the feet.

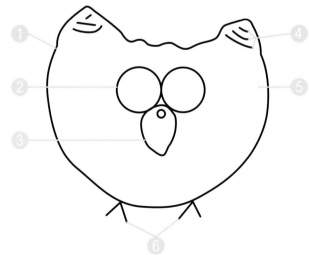

BEADED LACE BIRD

Recipe

1. Place lace bird on fabric.

2. Stack: size 4 opaque black seed bead topped with size 11 clear silver-lined seed bead for the bird's eye.

3. Backstitch: size 10 opaque yellow seed beads for the beak.

4. Backstitch: size 11 matte silver-lined orange seed beads to outline the body.

5. Backstitch: size 10 blue mix seed beads to outline the wings.

Ingredients

lace bird

size 4 opaque black seed bead

size 11 clear silver-lined seed bead

size 10 opaque yellow seed beads

size 11 matte silver-lined orange seed beads

size 10 blue mix seed beads

UNDER WATER

Contributed by Gail Smith

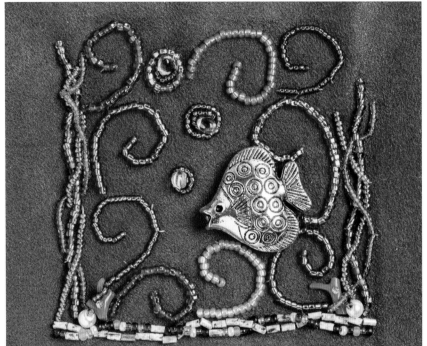

Recipe

1. Sand: backstitch with yellow bugles, size 11 brown mix seed beads, and 4mm glass pearls.

2. Bubbles: single bead stitch with 4mm clear glass drops, backstitch with size 15 blue zircon seed beads, size 15 silver-lined teal seed beads, and size 11 blue mix seed beads.

3. Stack: pieces of coral with clear seed bead.

4. Seaweed: backstitch and loops with size 15 chartreuse seed beads and size 11 green mix seed beads.

5. Seawater: backstitch with size 11 blue mix seed beads, size 15 blue zircon seed beads, and size 15 silver-lined teal seed beads.

6. Fish: metallic silver focal fish bead.

Ingredients

yellow bugles

size 11 brown mix seed beads

4mm glass pearls

4mm clear glass drops

size 15 blue zircon seed beads

size 15 silver-lined teal seed beads

size 11 blue mix seed beads

pieces of coral

size 15 clear seed beads

size 15 chartreuse seed beads

size 11 green mix seed beads

size 11 blue mix seed beads

metallic silver focal fish bead

Recipe

1. Backstitch: alternating size 11 matte silver-lined dark topaz seed beads and size 11 matte silver-lined orange seed beads.

2. Stack: size 4 metallic gold seed bead topped with size 8 opaque black seed bead to create eye.

3. Backstitch: alternating size 11 matte silver-lined dark topaz seed beads and size 11 matte silver-lined orange seed beads.

4. Backstitch: size 11 matte silver-lined orange seed beads.

5. Stack: orange shell sequins topped with size 15 silver-lined dark gold seed beads to create fish scales.

6. Stacks: size 8 clear silver-lined seed beads topped with size 15 clear silver-lined seed beads to create bubbles.

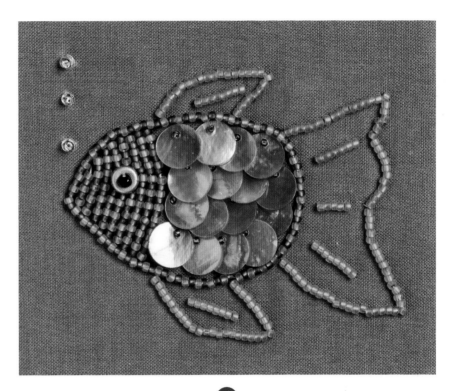

When stitching the overlapping shell sequins, it's easier to work from the bottom up.

Ingredients

size 11 matte silver-lined dark topaz seed beads

size 11 matte silver-lined orange seed beads

size 4 metallic gold seed bead

size 8 opaque black seed bead

orange shell sequins

size 15 silver-lined dark gold seed beads

size 8 clear silver-lined seed beads

size 15 clear silver-lined seed beads

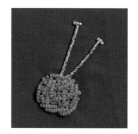

Symbols and Objects

Everyday objects make good subjects for embroidery, as do various popular symbols and icons. I like to stitch hats and shoes and make brooches with them. I've also included a couple of seasonal items in this chapter.

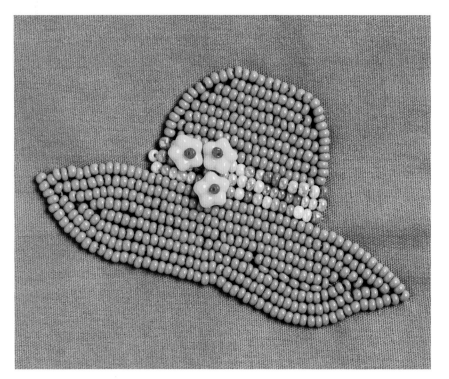

Recipe

1. Backstitch: size 10 multicolor pearl-finish seed beads to form band around hat.

2. Backstitch outline: size 10 opaque turquoise seed beads to create edge of hat.

3. Backstitch filling: size 10 opaque turquoise seed beads to fill in hat.

4. Stacks: yellow glass flowers topped with size 11 opaque red seed beads to add flowers to hat band.

Ingredients

size 10 multicolor pearl-finish seed beads

size 10 opaque turquoise seed beads

yellow glass flowers

size 11 opaque red seed beads

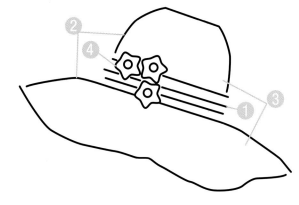

Recipe

1. Backstitch: alternating size 11 opaque black and metallic gold seed beads to create outline of shoe.

2. Stack: small black felt flower topped with size 8 metallic gold seed bead to add flower at top of shoe.

3. Stack: black felt flower and small tan felt flower topped with size 11 metallic gold seed bead to form floral embellishment near toe.

Ingredients

size 11 opaque black seed beads

size 11 metallic gold seed beads

small black felt flower

size 8 metallic gold seed bead

small tan felt flower

medium black felt flower

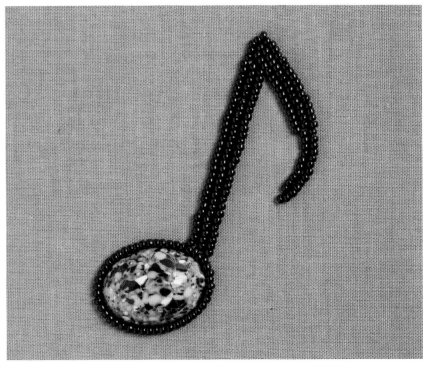

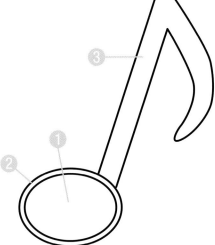

Ingredients

24 x 18mm acrylic cabochon

fabric glue

size 11 opaque black seed beads

Recipe

1. Glue 24 x 18mm acrylic cabochon to fabric.

2, 3. Backstitch: size 11 opaque black seed beads to create musical note.

Recipe

1, 2. Backstitch: size 8 matte silver-lined red seed beads alternating with size 8 metallic gold seed beads.

3, 4. Backstitch: size 8 matte silver-lined green seed beads alternating with size 8 metallic gold seed beads.

5. Backstitch: size 10 metallic silver seed beads.

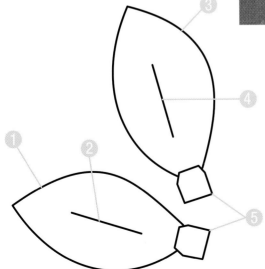

Ingredients

size 8 matte silver-lined red seed beads

size 8 metallic gold seed beads

size 8 matte silver-lined green seed beads

size 10 metallic silver seed beads

Recipe

1. Arrange blue and red half-oval felt shapes with a slight overlap.

2. Stacks: size 6 opaque black seed beads with size 10 clear silver-lined seed beads to create eyes.

3. Backstitch: size 10 clear silver-lined seed beads to create mouths.

4. Backstitch: size 11 opaque black seed beads to form ties.

Ingredients

blue and red half-oval felt shapes

size 6 opaque black seed beads

size 10 clear silver-lined seed beads

size 11 opaque black seed beads

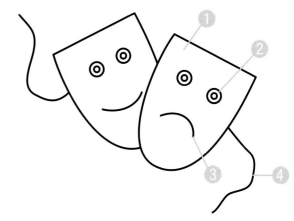

Recipe

1. Glue 18mm round dichroic glass cabochon to fabric to create center of bow.

2, 3. Backstitch: size 10 opaque light blue seed beads.

4. Backstitch: size 10 opaque blue seed beads.

Ingredients

18mm round dichroic glass cabochon

fabric glue

size 10 opaque light blue seed beads

size 10 opaque blue seed beads

Recipe

1. Backstitch: size 11 metallic silver cylinder beads to form knitting needles.

2. Loops: size 10 light red seed beads to create ball of yarn.

Ingredients

size 11 metallic silver cylinder beads

size 10 light red seed beads

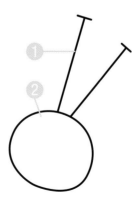

LADY IN A DRESS

Recipe

1, 2. Backstitch: mix of size 10 clear seed beads in various colors.

3. Single bead stitch: 14mm round flat millefiori glass bead.

4. Backstitch: mix of size 10 clear seed beads in various colors.

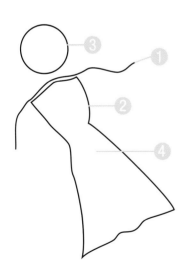

Ingredients

mix of size 10 clear seed beads in various colors

14mm round flat millefiori glass bead

Recipe

1. Stacks: size 6 matte orange AB seed beads topped with size 10 matte orange AB seed beads.

2. Stacks: size 6 matte orange AB seed beads topped with size 10 metallic gold seed beads.

Ingredients

size 6 matte orange AB seed beads

size 10 matte orange AB seed beads

size 10 metallic gold seed beads

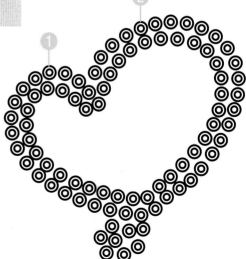

UMBRELLA

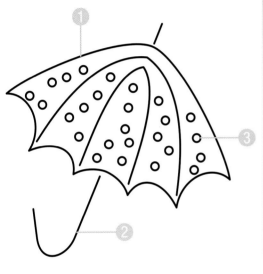

Recipe

1. Stacks: size 8 silver-lined dark topaz AB seed beads topped with size 15 silver-lined transparent gold seed beads.

2. Backstitch: size 10 metallic gold seed beads.

3. Scatter stitch: size 15 silver-lined transparent gold seed beads.

Ingredients

size 8 silver-lined dark topaz AB seed beads

size 15 silver-lined transparent gold seed beads

size 10 metallic gold seed beads

size 15 silver-lined transparent gold seed beads

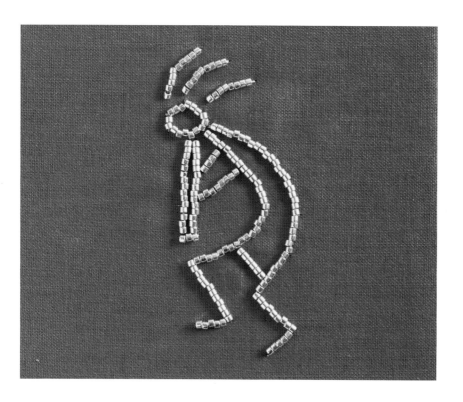

Ingredients

size 11 metallic silver cylinder beads

Recipe

1, 2, 3, 4, 5. Backstitch: size 11 metallic silver cylinder beads to create entire figure.

CUPCAKE

Recipe

1, 2. Backstitch: size 11 metallic copper seed beads to form cupcake liner.

3. Backstitch: size 10 metallic silver seed beads to create cupcake frosting.

4. Stacks: size 6 metallic copper seed beads topped with size 10 metallic silver seed beads.

5. Scatter stitch: size 10 metallic silver seed beads.

6. Single bead stitch: Orange shell bead to embellish top of cupcake.

Ingredients

size 11 metallic copper seed beads

size 10 metallic silver seed beads

size 6 metallic copper seed beads

orange shell bead

Monograms

Bead-stitched monograms are great for personalizing stitched items like quilts. They also make wonderful presents, either as small framed pieces or as jewelry. For example, a framed piece featuring the initials of the couple makes a nice wedding present. Each design in this section demonstrates a beading and letter style. Follow the examples to bead other letters of your choice in similar styles.

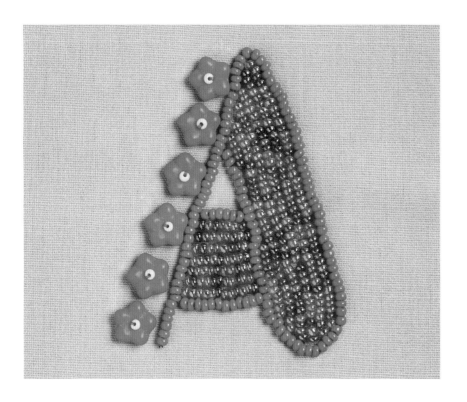

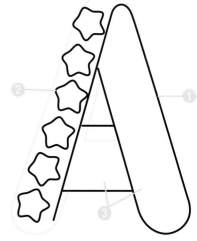

Ingredients

size 10 opaque red seed beads

red flower beads

size 11 light pink seed beads

size 10 transparent red mix seed beads

Recipe

1. Backstitch: size 10 opaque red seed beads.

2. Stack stitch: red flower beads topped with size 11 light pink seed beads.

3. Backstitch: size 10 transparent red mix seed beads.

Recipe

1. Backstitch: 10mm flat round green shell beads alternating with size 11 metallic dark green iris seed beads to create left side of letter.

2, 3, 4. Backstitch: size 8 metallic dark green iris seed beads.

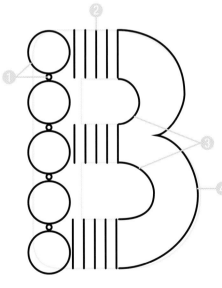

Ingredients

10mm flat round green shell beads

size 11 metallic dark green iris seed beads

size 8 metallic dark green iris seed beads

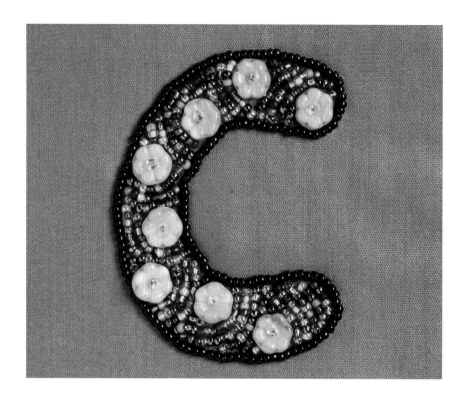

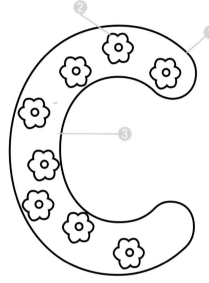

Ingredients

size 11 opaque black seed beads

yellow-orange flower beads

size 11 clear seed beads

size 11 blue mix seed beads

Recipe

1. Backstitch: size 11 opaque black seed beads to outline letter.

2. Stack stitch: yellow-orange flower beads topped with size 11 clear seed beads to embellish C.

3. Backstitch: size 11 blue mix seed beads to fill in letter.

For the blue seed beads, first stitch curved lines that extend from one side to the other, and then go back and fill in the holes.

DELTA

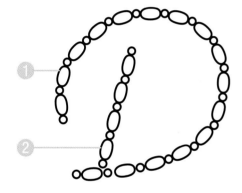

Recipe

1, 2. Backstitch: alternating size 10 pearl-finish seed beads, and 5mm rice-shaped cat's eye glass beads to create the entire letter.

Ingredients

size 10 pearl-finish seed beads

5mm rice-shaped cat's eye glass beads

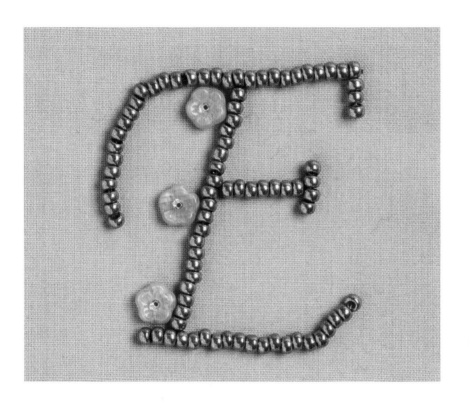

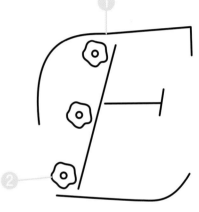

Ingredients

size 8 metallic pink seed beads

pink flowers

size 15 clear silver-lined seed beads

Recipe

1. Backstitch: size 8 metallic pink seed beads to form letter E.

2. Stacks: pink flowers topped with size 15 clear silver-lined seed beads to embellish left side of letter.

Recipe

1, 3, 5, 7. Backstitch: size 8 matte transparent teal AB seed beads.

2, 4, 6, 8. Backstitch: size 8 matte transparent topaz AB seed beads.

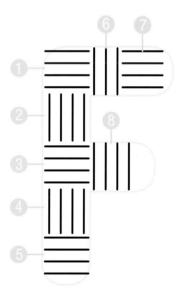

As you stitch this basketweave pattern, be prepared to change the number of beads or the number of rows as you go, to accommodate the slight differences in bead sizes.

Ingredients

size 8 matte transparent teal AB seed beads

size 8 matte transparent topaz AB seed beads

Ingredients

10mm burgundy dyed flat shell beads

size 11 pink mix seed beads

Recipe

1. Single bead stitch: 10mm burgundy dyed flat shell beads.

2. Five-bead loops: size 11 pink mix seed beads.

The loops are stitched very close together, in random directions. For an interesting texture, vary the distance between where you come up through the fabric and where you go back down to create loops of different heights.

Recipe

1. Backstitch: size 10 metallic blue iris seed beads to outline letter.

2. Stacks: metallic blue iris triangle beads topped with size 11 metallic gold seed beads to embellish inside of letter.

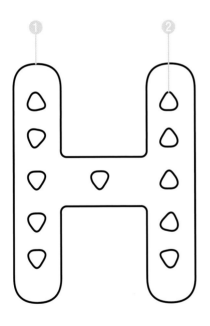

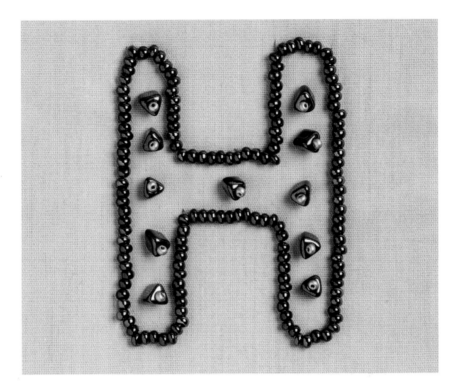

Ingredients

size 10 metallic blue iris seed beads

metallic blue iris triangle beads

size 11 metallic gold seed beads

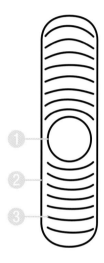

Ingredients

small dichroic glass cabochon

fabric glue

size 8 turquoise mix seed beads

Recipe

1. Glue small dichroic glass cabochon to fabric.

2, 3. Backstitch: size 8 turquoise mix seed beads around glass bead in the shape of the letter I.

Using seed bead mixes is an easy way to add interest to a piece.

JULIETT

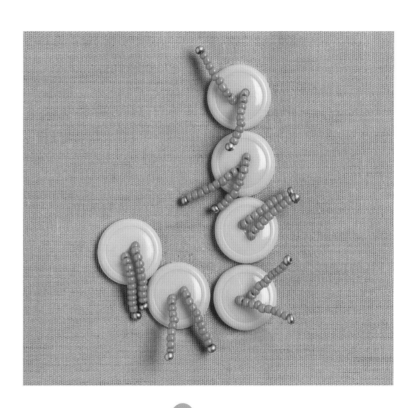

Recipe

1. Arrange yellow buttons in J shape.

2. Stacks in each hole in the buttons: ten size 10 opaque orange seed beads topped with size 10 metallic gold seed beads.

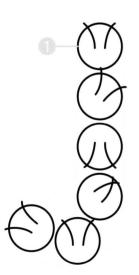

When going down through the stack of beads, be careful not to split the thread with your needle.

Ingredients

yellow buttons, ½" (1.3cm)

size 10 opaque orange seed beads

size 10 metallic gold seed beads

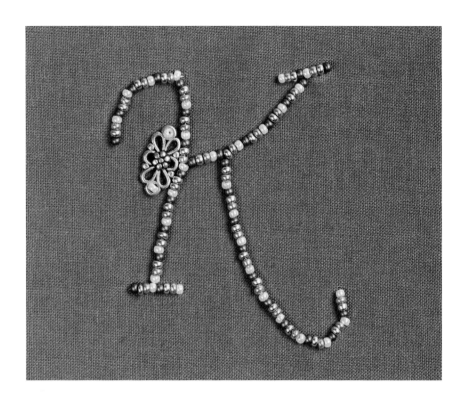

Ingredients

size 11 metallic copper seed beads

size 10 metallic silver seed beads

size 11 metallic gold seed beads

size 10 pearl-finish seed beads

silver filigree piece

Recipe

1. Backstitch: alternating size 11 metallic copper, size 10 metallic silver, size 11 metallic gold, and size 10 pearl-finish seed beads, create letter K.

2. Stacks: size 10 pearl-finish seed beads worked in the holes of a silver filigree piece.

Some size 10 seed beads and size 11 beads are very close in size, so that they can be used together.

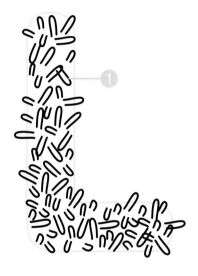

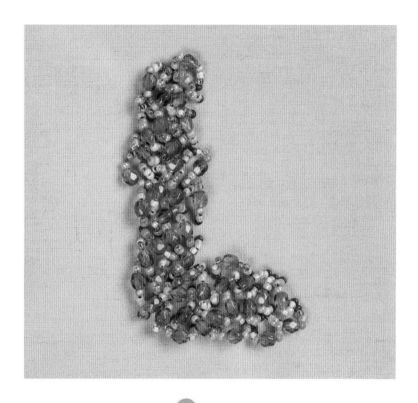

Recipe

1. Create loops consisting of nine beads: One size 11 opaque dark brown seed bead, three size 11 orange mix seed beads, one 4mm red-orange fire-polish faceted round bead, three size 11 orange mix seed beads, and one size 11 opaque dark brown seed bead.

The dark brown beads at the beginning and end of each loop help give depth to the design, and the fire-polish bead adds some sparkle.

Ingredients

size 11 opaque dark brown seed beads

size 11 orange mix seed beads

4mm red-orange fire-polish faceted round beads

size 11 orange mix seed beads

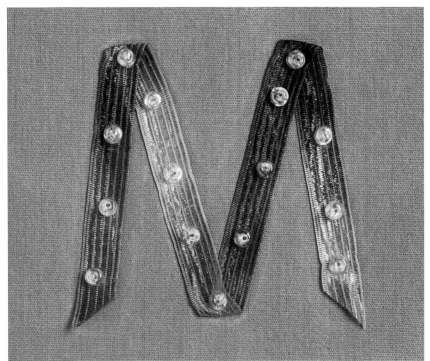

Use transparent beads when you want to show off the color of the fabric underneath.

Recipe

1. Arrange variegated ribbon yarn in shape of the letter M.

2. Stack stitch: size 6 clear AB seed beads topped with size 11 clear AB seed beads to embellish letter.

Ingredients

variegated ribbon yarn

size 6 clear AB seed beads

size 11 clear AB seed beads

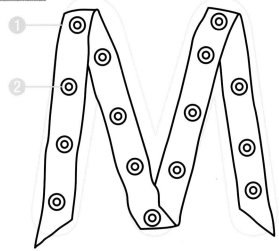

Recipe

1. Stacks: purple triangle beads topped with size 11 opaque yellow seed beads to create the outline of the letter.

2. Stacks: yellow glass flower beads topped with size 10 matte purple AB seed beads to form the remaining outline.

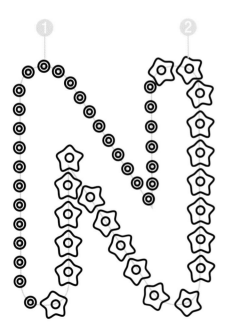

Ingredients

purple triangle beads

size 11 opaque yellow seed beads

yellow glass flower beads

size 10 matte purple AB seed beads

OSCAR

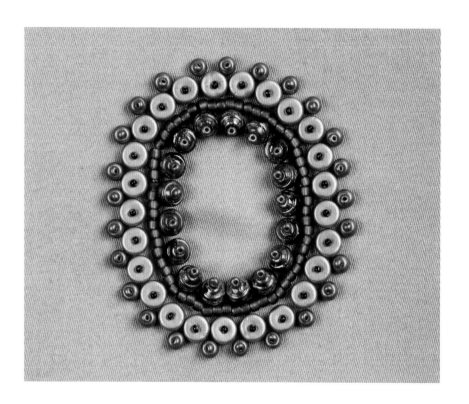

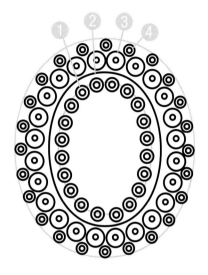

Ingredients

round copper and black beads

size 11 metallic copper seed beads

size 8 matte silver-lined dark topaz
seed beads

round flat 4mm metal beads with
copper finish

size 15 opaque black seed beads

size 6 metallic copper seed beads

Recipe

1. Stacks: round copper and black beads topped
with size 11 metallic copper seed beads.

2. Backstitch: size 8 matte silver-lined dark topaz
seed beads.

3. Stacks: round flat 4mm metal beads with
copper finish topped with size 15 opaque black
seed beads.

4. Stacks: size 6 metallic copper seed beads
topped with size 11 metallic copper seed beads.

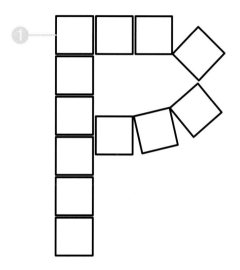

Recipe

1. Single bead stitch: 8mm square millefiori glass beads in a variety of colors to create letter.

Ingredients

8mm square millefiori glass beads in a variety of colors

Recipe

1. Stacks: pink felt flowers topped with size 6 metallic silver seed beads, and size 11 clear silver-lined seed beads to form tail of Q.

2. Stacks: size 6 metallic silver seed beads topped with size 11 clear silver-lined seed beads to outline letter.

Ingredients

pink felt flowers

size 6 metallic silver seed beads

size 11 clear silver-lined seed beads

ROMEO

Contributed by Rose Klein

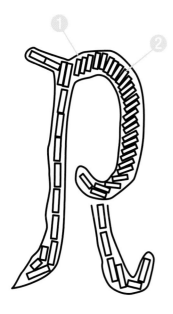

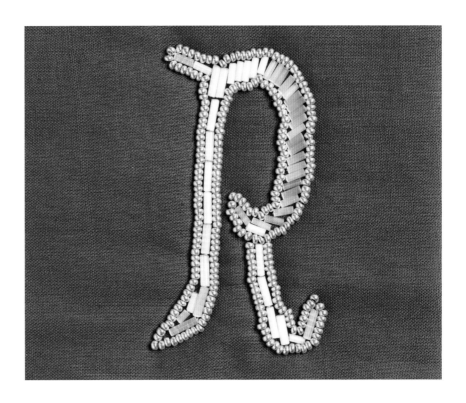

Recipe

1. Backstitch: size 11 metallic gold seed beads to create outline of letter R.

2. White satin bugle beads stitched with a combination of couching and satin stitch to fill in letter.

Ingredients

size 11 metallic gold seed beads

white satin bugle beads

Ingredients

size 8 opaque orange, yellow, and
green seed beads

Recipe

1. Backstitch: alternating size 8 opaque orange,
yellow, and green seed beads to form outline of
letter S.

TANGO

Recipe

1, 2, 3. Backstitch: alternate 6mm clear green acrylic bicones with size 10 metallic gold seed beads to create letter T.

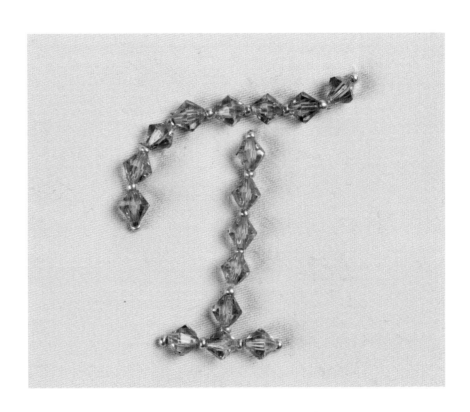

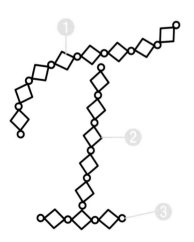

Ingredients

6mm clear green acrylic bicones

size 10 metallic gold seed beads

Ingredients

size 8 silver-lined dark topaz seed beads

size 8 matte silver-lined dark topaz seed beads

Recipe

1. Backstitch: size 8 silver-lined dark topaz seed beads.

2. Backstitch: size 8 matte silver-lined dark topaz seed beads.

In both the U and the V, I use beads of the same color but with different finishes. This adds an interesting texture to the work.

VICTOR

Recipe

1. Backstitch alternating lines: size 11 opaque orange seed beads and size 10 clear silver-lined orange seed beads to form letter V.

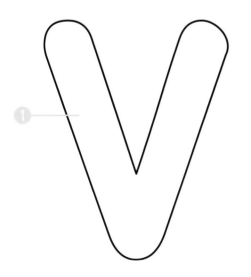

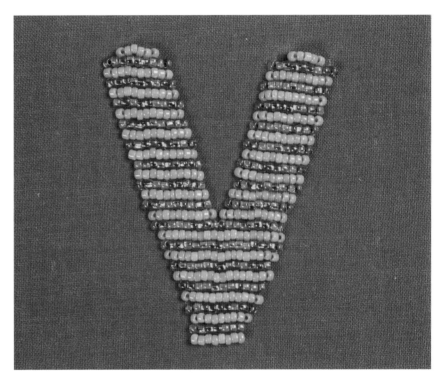

Ingredients

size 11 opaque orange seed beads

size 10 clear silver-lined orange seed beads

WHISKEY

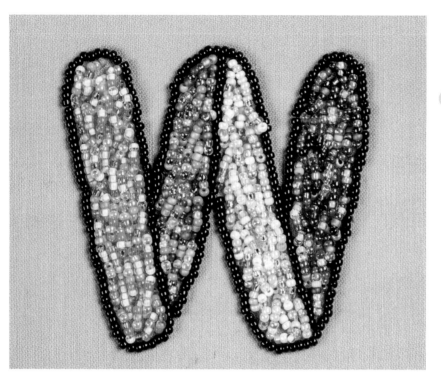

Ingredients

size 11 opaque black seed beads

size 11 orange mix seed beads

size 11 turquoise mix seed beads

size 11 yellow mix seed beads

size 11 purple mix seed beads

Recipe

1. Backstitch: size 11 opaque black seed beads to outline letter.

2. Shallow loops: size 11 orange mix seed beads to fill.

3. Shallow loops: size 11 turquoise mix seed beads to fill.

4. Shallow loops: size 11 yellow mix seed beads to fill.

5. Shallow loops: size 11 purple mix seed beads to fill.

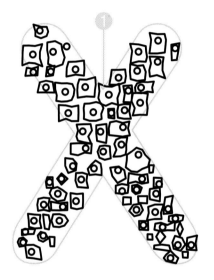

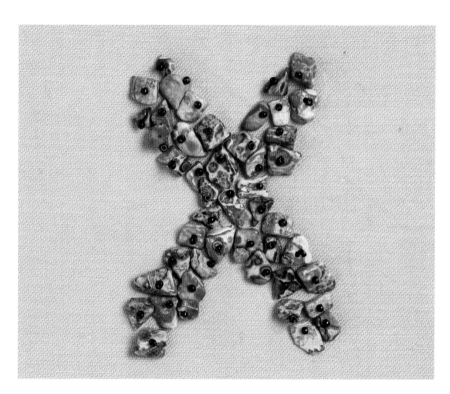

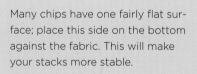

Many chips have one fairly flat surface; place this side on the bottom against the fabric. This will make your stacks more stable.

Recipe

1. Stacks: pink and grey stone chips topped with size 15 opaque black seed beads to form letter X.

Ingredients

pink and grey stone chips

size 15 opaque black seed beads

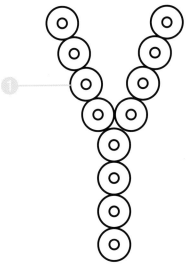

Ingredients

8–10mm glass nuggets in orange and green colors

size 11 metallic gold seed beads

Recipe

1. Stacks: 8–10mm glass nuggets in orange and green colors topped with size 11 metallic gold seed beads to form letter Y.

Recipe

1. Backstitch: 4mm black AB drops to create letter Z.

As you get used to working with the drops, you'll find that they fall in line fairly easily.

Ingredients

4mm black AB drops

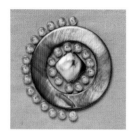

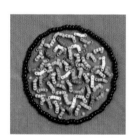

Circular Designs

Circular, symmetrical designs, also called mandalas, can be found around the globe in the art of various cultures. Circular designs appear in architectural and decorative elements, in needlework like lace and crochet, in textiles, and in nature, as in flowers and snowflakes.

The designs in this chapter are inspired by mandalas. For some of them, I use a design tool I created called Geneviève's Mandala Stencils to make sure the image is symmetrical. See page 126 to learn more about these stencils.

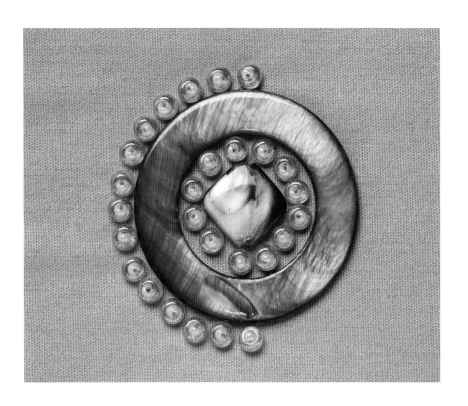

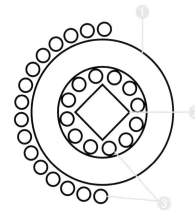

Ingredients

brown shell circular frame bead

brown square shell bead

size 6 clear seed beads

size 11 pearl-finish seed beads

Recipe

1. Single bead stitch: brown shell circular frame bead.

2. Single bead stitch: brown square shell bead.

3. Stacks: size 6 clear seed beads, topped with size 11 pearl-finish seed beads.

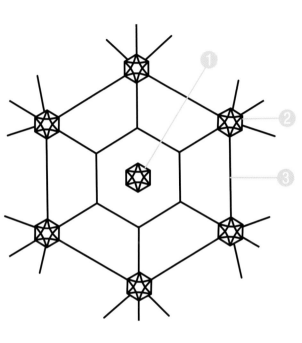

Recipe

1. Single bead stitch: 8mm round faceted clear AB crystal to form center of design.

2, 3. Backstitch : size 8 opaque white seed beads, with 6mm round faceted clear AB crystal at the outside intersections to create snowflake.

Ingredients

8mm round faceted clear AB crystal

size 8 opaque white seed beads

six 6mm round faceted clear AB crystals

Ingredients

size 6 multicolor AB seed beads

size 11 metallic gold seed beads

multicolor AB flowers

Recipe

1. Stacks: size 6 multicolor AB seed beads topped with size 11 metallic gold seed beads to form outer circle.

2. Stacks: multicolor AB flowers topped with size 11 metallic gold seed beads to create center design.

CIRCULAR 4

Recipe

1. Paint wood donut shape with DecoArt Black Pearl acrylic paint and glue to fabric.

2. Loops: size 10 opaque red seed beads.

3. Stitch silver and red shank button into the center of the donut.

4. Stacks: size 6 gunmetal seed beads topped with size 10 opaque red seed beads.

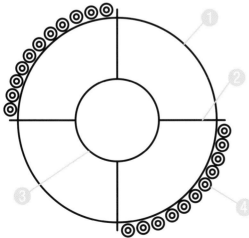

Ingredients

wood donut shape

DecoArt Black Pearl acrylic paint

paint brush

fabric glue

size 10 opaque red seed beads

silver and red shank button

size 6 gunmetal seed beads

CIRCULAR 5

Recipe

1. Stack: size 4 metallic gold seed bead topped with size 8 metallic gold seed bead.

2. Stacks: size 11 metallic gold seed bead worked in the holes of gold-tone chandelier earring findings.

3. Stacks: size 6 metallic gold seed beads topped with size 10 metallic gold seed beads.

4. Backstitch: one size 15 metallic gold seed bead, one 4mm red crystal bicone, and one size 15 metallic gold seed bead.

Ingredients

size 4 metallic gold seed bead

size 8 metallic gold seed bead

size 11 metallic gold seed bead

gold-tone chandelier earring findings

size 6 metallic gold seed beads

size 10 metallic gold seed beads

size 15 metallic gold seed beads

4mm red crystal bicones

CIRCULAR 6

Recipe

1. Backstitch: size 8 opaque black seed beads to create outline.

2. Seven-bead loops: size 11 opaque white, yellow, red, light purple, light green, orange, and light blue seed beads to fill center.

3. Scatter stitch: size 11 clear AB seed beads to embellish.

Ingredients

size 8 opaque black seed beads

size 11 opaque white, yellow, red, light purple, light green, orange, and light blue seed beads

size 11 clear AB seed beads

CIRCULAR 7

Ingredients

10mm flat round dyed turquoise shell bead

metallic silver bugles

size 10 metallic silver seed beads

eight 4mm magenta firepolish crystals

eight size 4 metallic silver beads

eight size 8 matte blue silver-lined seed beads

Recipe

1. Single bead stitch: 10mm flat round dyed turquoise shell bead for center.

2. Backstitch: metallic silver bugles and size 10 metallic silver seed beads.

3. Backstitch: five size 10 metallic silver seed beads, one 4mm magenta firepolish crystal, and five size 10 metallic silver seed beads.

4. Stacks: size 4 metallic silver beads topped with size 8 matte blue silver-lined seed beads.

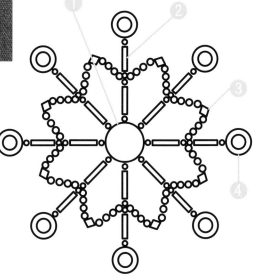

SOUTHWEST SUNFLOWER

Contributed by Roxann Blazetich-Ozols

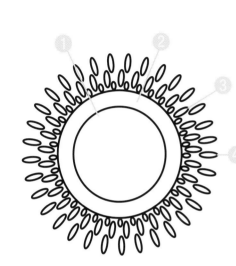

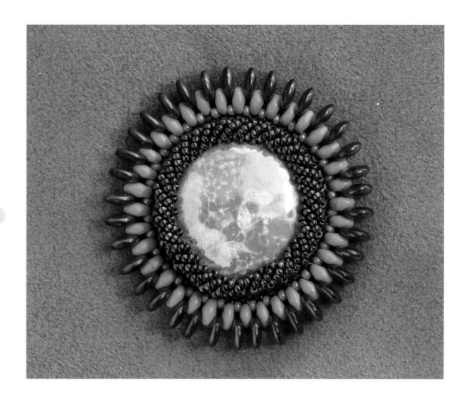

Recipe

1. Glue round ceramic cabochon to fabric.

2. Peyote bezel: size 11 matte brown cylinder beads; small loops at the top of the bezel with size 15 metallic brown seed beads.

3. Backstitch: alternating size 13 turquoise charlottes and turquoise twins.

4. Backstitch through the second hole in the twins, alternating with 6mm top-drilled copper-finish lentil beads.

Ingredients

round ceramic cabochon

fabric glue

size 11 matte brown cylinder beads

size 15 metallic brown seed beads

size 13 turquoise charlottes

turquoise twins

6mm top-drilled copper-finish lentil beads

Recipe

1. Paint a 1½" (3.8cm) domed wood piece with DecoArt Metallic Copper acrylic paint and glue to the fabric.

2. Backstitch, alternating size 8 opaque black seed beads with 15mm long metallic copper finish daggers.

Ingredients

1½" (3.8cm) domed wood piece

DecoArt Metallic Copper acrylic paint

paint brush

fabric glue

size 8 opaque black seed beads

15mm long metallic copper-finish daggers

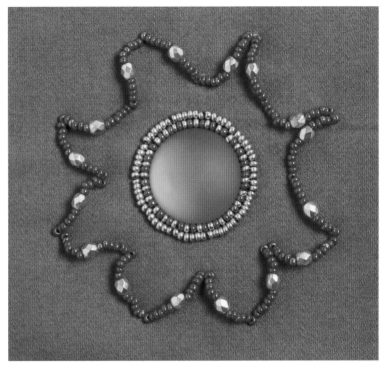

Recipe

1. Glue dark pink lucite cabochon to fabric.

2. Backstitch, alternating size 10 metallic gold seed beads and size 10 dark red AB seed beads.

3. Backstitch: size 10 metallic gold seed beads.

4. Loops consisting of six size 10 dark red AB seed beads, one 3mm gold fire-polish crystal, and six size 10 dark red AB seed beads.

Ingredients

dark pink lucite cabochon

fabric glue

size 10 metallic gold seed beads

size 10 dark red AB seed beads

3mm gold fire-polish crystals

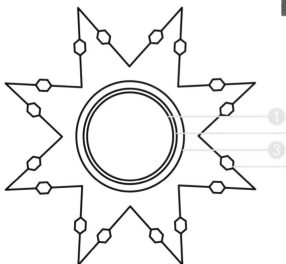

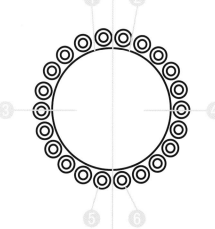

Ingredients

size 10 metallic gold seed beads

size 10 opaque dark blue seed beads

size 11 yellow mix seed beads

size 11 blue mix seed beads

size 6 metallic gold seed beads

size 6 opaque dark blue seed beads

Recipe

1. Backstitch: size 10 metallic gold seed beads.

2. Backstitch: size 10 opaque dark blue seed beads.

3. Shallow loops: size 11 yellow mix seed beads.

4. Shallow loops: size 11 blue mix seed beads.

5. Stacks: size 6 metallic gold seed beads topped with size 10 opaque dark blue seed beads.

6. Stacks: size 6 opaque dark blue seed beads topped with size 10 metallic gold seed beads.

Recipe

1. Glue 54mm diameter wood donut to fabric.

2. Glue metallic silver sun charm to donut.

3. Stacks: size 6 metallic silver seed beads topped with size 11 metallic copper seed beads.

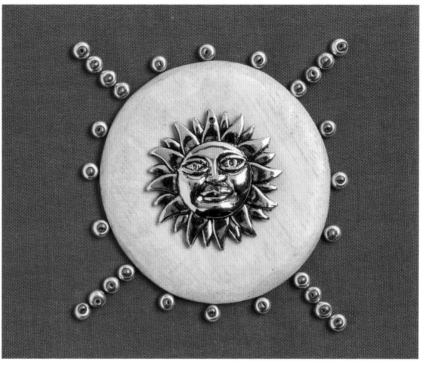

Ingredients

wood donut, 54mm diameter

fabric glue

metallic silver sun charm

size 6 metallic silver seed beads

size 11 metallic copper seed beads

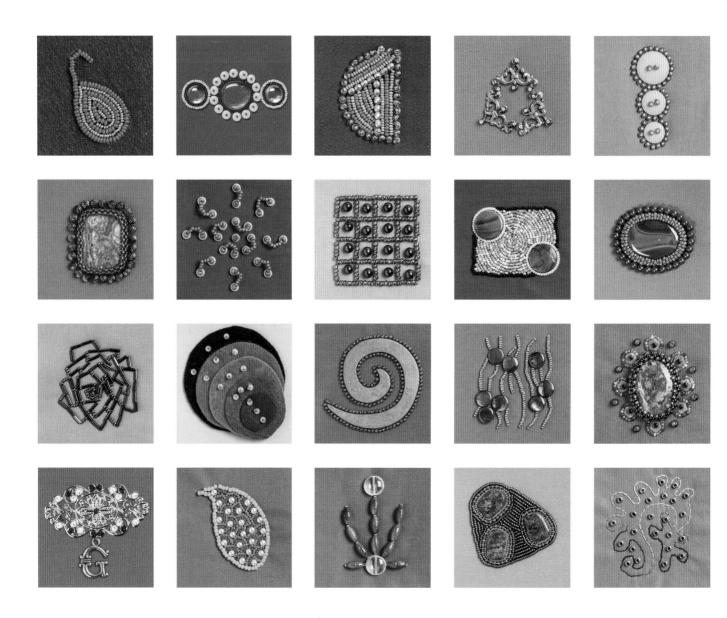

Abstract Designs

Abstract designs allow your imagination to have free rein. I hope some of the ideas here will inspire you to create new designs of your own.

ABSTRACT 1

Recipe

1. Backstitch: size 8 opaque red seed beads.

2. Backstitch: size 11 metallic gold seed beads.

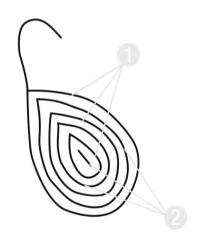

Ingredients

size 8 opaque red seed beads

size 11 metallic gold seed beads

Start from the outline, and stitch the beads from the outside in. Since you have to alternate colors, you may find it easiest to use two needles with two colors of thread.

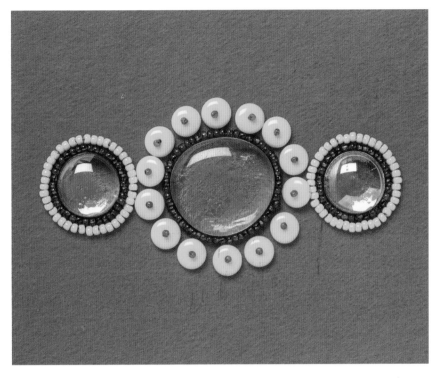

Recipe

1. Glue small clear glass cabochons to fabric.

2. Backstitch circle of size 8 red transparent seed beads.

3. Backstitch circle of size 8 opaque yellow seed beads.

4. Glue large clear glass cabochon to fabric.

5. Backstitch circle of size 8 red transparent seed beads.

6. Stacks: flat yellow bead topped with size 11 red seed beads.

Ingredients

small clear glass cabochons

fabric glue

size 8 red transparent seed beads

size 8 opaque yellow seed beads

large clear glass cabochon

flat yellow beads

size 11 red seed beads

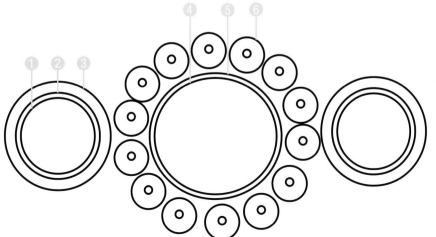

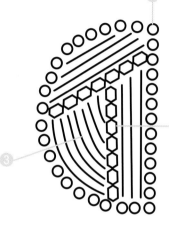

Ingredients

size 6 clear seed beads

size 11 metallic gold seed beads

4mm gold fire-polished oval beads

size 10 opaque red seed beads

size 11 opaque light blue seed beads

Recipe

1. Stacks: size 6 clear seed beads topped with size 11 metallic gold seed beads.

2. Backstitch: 4mm gold fire-polished oval beads.

3. Backstitch: alternate lines of size 10 opaque red and size 11 opaque light blue seed beads.

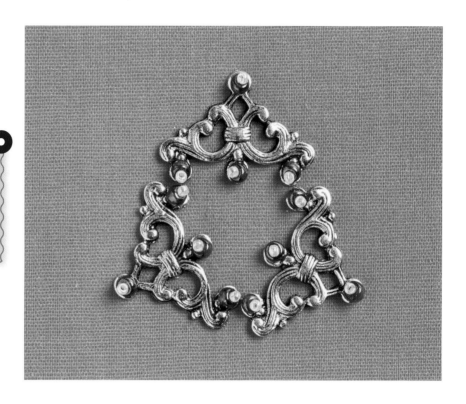

Chandelier earring findings come in a wide variety of shapes and finishes. They can add a nice metallic touch to your designs.

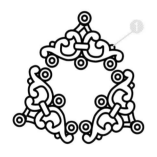

Recipe

1. Stacks: size 8 silver-lined dark topaz AB seed beads worked in the holes of silver chandelier earring findings.

Ingredients

size 8 silver-lined dark topaz AB seed beads

three silver chandelier earring findings

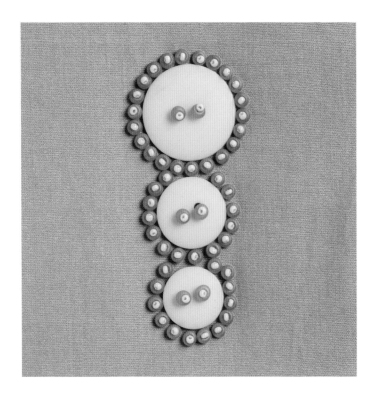

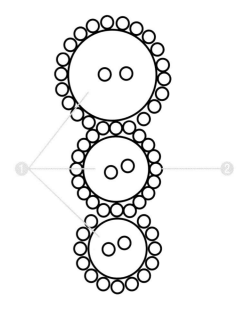

Ingredients

three pink buttons in 25mm, 18mm, 16mm diameters

size 6 matte dark pink seed beads

size 11 opaque light pink seed beads

Recipe

1. Stacks: three pink buttons. In each button hole, stack size 6 matte dark pink seed bead topped with size 11 opaque light pink seed bead.

2. Stacks: size 6 matte dark pink seed beads, topped with size 11 opaque light pink seed beads.

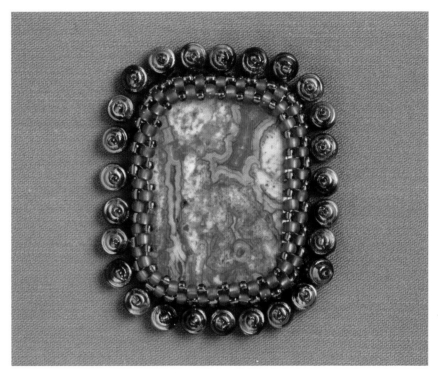

Recipe

1. Glue turquoise rectangular flat bead to fabric.

2. Peyote bezel around the bead: size 8 silver-lined matte blue seed beads and size 8 and 11 silver-lined dark topaz seed beads.

3. Stack stitch: round copper and black beads topped with size 11 silver-lined dark topaz seed beads.

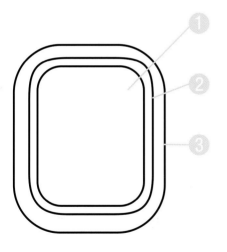

Turquoise and orange/copper are complementary colors, meaning they are on opposite sides of the color wheel. Try other combinations of complementary colors in your work.

Ingredients

turquoise rectangular flat bead

fabric glue

size 8 silver-lined matte blue seed beads

size 8 silver-lined dark topaz seed beads

size 11 silver-lined dark topaz seed beads

round copper and black beads

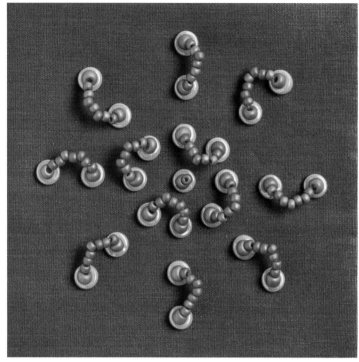

Recipe

1. Stack: a 6mm pearl-finish donut bead topped with a size 6 matte opaque green AB seed bead and a size 8 matte opaque green AB seed bead.

2. Loops: one 6mm pearl-finish donut bead, one size 6 matte opaque green AB seed bead, seven size 8 matte opaque green AB seed bead, one size 6 matte opaque green AB seed bead, and one 6mm pearl-finish donut bead.

Ingredients

6mm pearl-finish donut beads

size 6 matte opaque green AB seed beads

size 8 matte opaque green AB seed beads

You'll find that it's better to use an odd number of beads in a loop, so that you have the center bead as a "point."

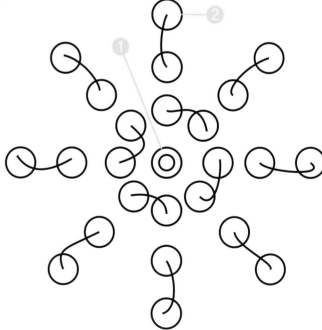

ABSTRACT 8

Recipe

1. Single bead stitch: 20mm flat grey shell beads.

2. Backstitch: size 11 pearl-finish seed beads.

3. Backstitch: size 11 opaque black seed beads for outline.

4. Backstitch: size 11 grey and pink mix seed beads. The beads are stitched in a spiral pattern beginning in the center. Fill the gaps left between the spiral and the black outline with size 15 clear silver-lined seed beads.

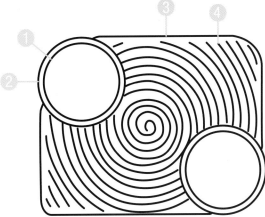

Ingredients

20mm flat grey shell beads

size 11 pearl-finish seed beads

size 11 opaque black seed beads

size 11 grey and pink mix seed beads

size 15 clear silver-lined seed beads

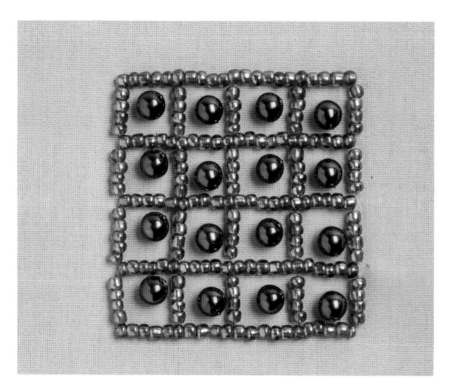

Ingredients

size 8 transparent gold AB seed
beads

brown glass pearls

Recipe

1. Backstitch: size 8 transparent gold AB seed
beads to outline design.

2. Single bead stitch: brown glass pearls in each
square.

ABSTRACT 10

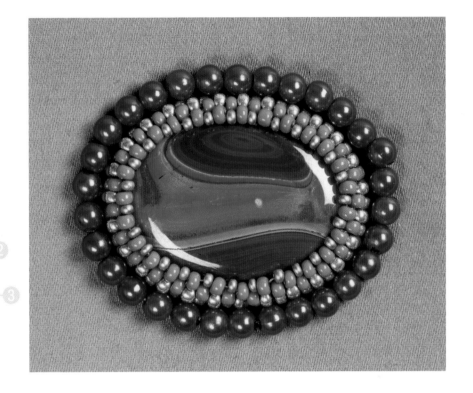

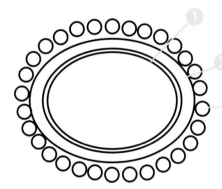

Recipe

1. Glue malachite cabochon to fabric.

2. Peyote bezel: size 8 opaque light green seed beads, size 8 metallic gold seed beads, and size 10 metallic gold seed beads.

3. Backstitch: 5mm green glass pearls.

Ingredients

malachite cabochon

fabric glue

size 8 opaque light green seed beads

size 8 metallic gold seed beads

size 10 metallic gold seed beads

5mm green glass pearls

ABSTRACT 11

Contributed by Rose Klein

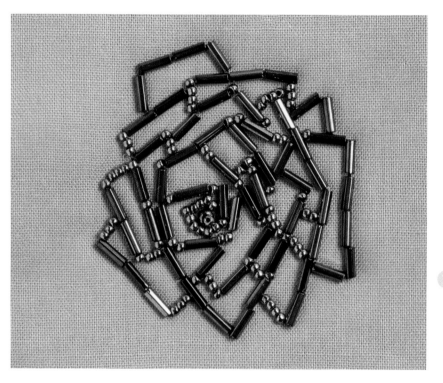

Ingredients

brown iris bugles

size 11 metallic copper seed beads

size 8 metallic copper seed bead

Recipe

1. Backstitch: brown iris bugles and size 11 metallic copper seed beads.

2. Stack: size 8 metallic copper seed bead topped with size 11 metallic copper seed bead.

Do not apply glue to areas that will be stitched, because it will be difficult to push the needle through the dried glue.

Recipe

1. Overlap slightly and glue five felt circles to fabric so they don't move when the beads are stitched.

2. Stacks: size 6 pearl-finish seed beads topped with size 11 metallic gold seed beads.

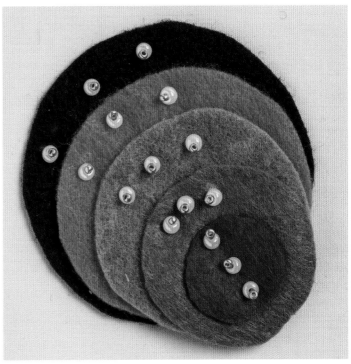

Ingredients

five felt circles in different sizes and colors

fabric glue

size 6 pearl-finish seed beads

size 11 metallic gold seed beads

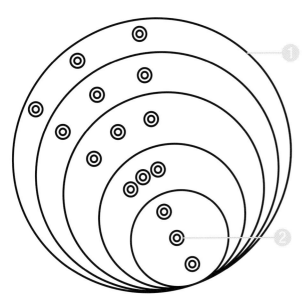

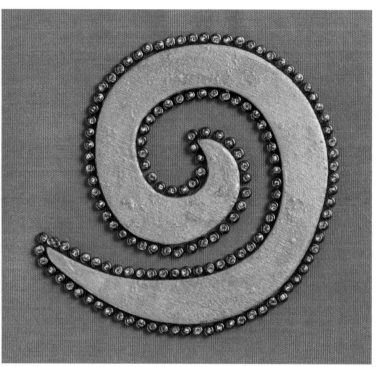

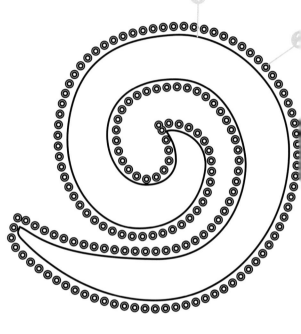

Ingredients

wood spiral shape

DecoArt Splendid Gold acrylic paint

paint brush

fabric glue

size 8 silver-lined dark topaz AB seed beads

size 15 silver-lined light gold seed beads

Recipe

1. Paint wood spiral shape with DecoArt Splendid Gold acrylic paint and glue to fabric.

2. Stacks: size 8 silver-lined dark topaz AB seed beads topped with size 15 silver-lined light gold seed beads.

ABSTRACT 14

Recipe

1. Single bead stitch: dyed shell 10mm disks.

2. Backstitch: size 10 metallic gold seed beads.

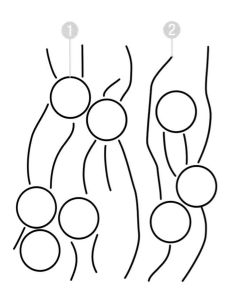

Ingredients

dyed shell 10mm disks

size 10 metallic gold seed beads

Ingredients

flat stone bead in pink and grey colors

fabric glue

size 8 gunmetal seed beads

size 8 dark rose silver-lined seed beads

size 11 transparent pink seed beads

pink glass flowers

size 15 opaque black seed beads

size 11 pink mix seed beads

size 6 gunmetal seed beads

Recipe

1. Glue flat stone bead to fabric.

2. Peyote bezel: size 8 gunmetal seed beads, size 8 dark rose silver-lined seed beads, and size 11 transparent pink seed beads.

3. Stacks: pink glass flower topped with size 8 gunmetal seed bead and size 15 opaque black seed bead.

4. Backstitch: size 11 pink mix seed beads.

5. Stacks: size 6 gunmetal seed bead topped with size 8 dark rose silver-lined seed bead.

Recipe

1. Glue letter charm to fabric.

2. Stitch down silver filigree with stacks: size 8 pearl-finish seed beads topped with size 15 clear silver-lined seed beads.

3. Stacks: size 8 opaque black seed beads topped with size 15 opaque black seed beads.

4. Stacks: size 6 opaque red seed beads topped with size 15 clear silver-lined seed beads.

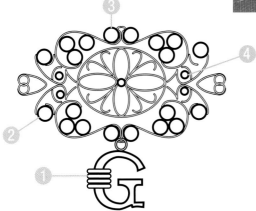

Ingredients

letter charm

fabric glue

silver filigree

size 8 pearl-finish seed beads

size 15 clear silver-lined seed beads

size 8 opaque black seed beads

size 15 opaque black seed beads

size 6 opaque red seed beads

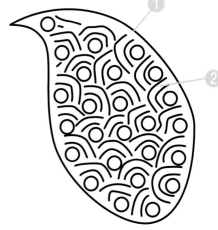

Ingredients

size 8 opaque yellow seed beads

3mm glass pearls

size 11 opaque red seed beads

size 11 opaque orange seed beads

Recipe

1. Backstitch: size 8 opaque yellow seed beads to create shape outline.

2. Each unit filling the shape is made up of one 3mm glass pearl, backstitched size 11 opaque red seed beads, and backstitched size 11 opaque orange seed beads.

Start from the bottom of the shape and work your way up.

ABSTRACT 18

Recipe

1. Single bead stitch: 12mm clear round glass beads.

2. Backstitch: 10mm acrylic blue and gold beads, alternating with size 10 metallic gold seed beads.

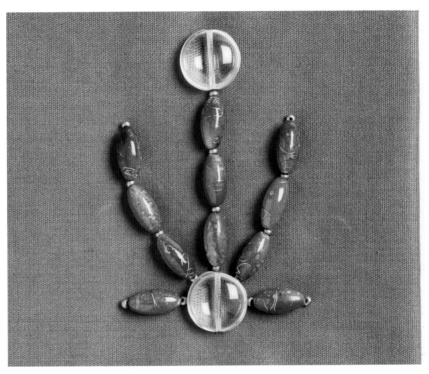

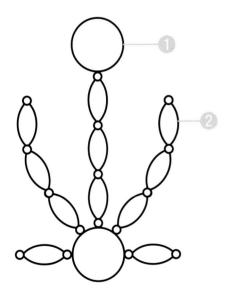

Ingredients

12mm clear round glass beads

10mm acrylic blue and gold beads

size 10 metallic gold seed beads

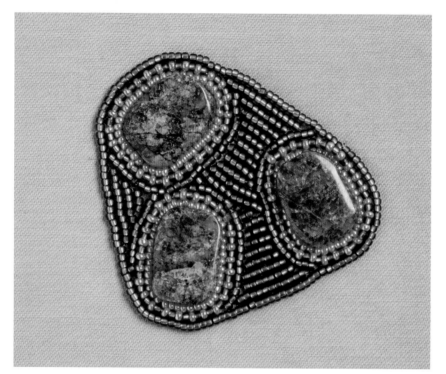

Recipe

1. Single bead stitch: green and coral stone beads.

2. Backstitch: size 11 coral pink pearl-finish seed beads.

3. Backstitch: size 11 matte silver-lined olive seed beads alternating with size 11 coral pink pearl-finish seed beads.

4, 5, 6. Backstitch: size 11 matte silver-lined olive seed beads.

Ingredients

green and coral stone beads

size 11 coral pink pearl-finish seed beads

size 11 matte silver-lined olive seed beads

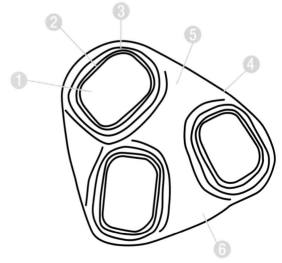

Recipe

1. Backstitch: three strands of variegated grey embroidery floss.

2. Stacks: size 6 metallic silver seed beads topped with size 15 opaque black seed beads.

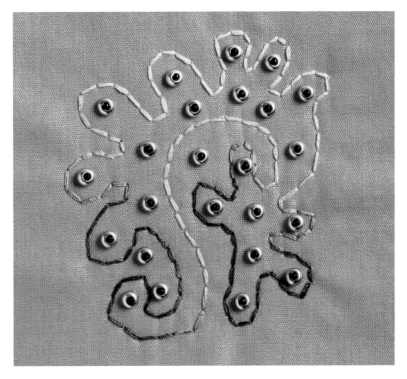

Ingredients

three strands of variegated grey embroidery floss

size 6 metallic silver seed beads

size 15 opaque black seed beads

Ingredients

size 11 opaque black seed beads

size 11 opaque white seed beads

Recipe

1, 2, 3. Backstitch: size 11 opaque black seed beads.

4. Backstitch: size 11 opaque white seed beads.

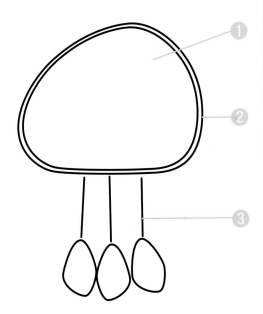

Recipe

1. Glue green stone cabochon to fabric.

2. Backstitch: size 8 transparent green AB seed beads.

3. Stack/fringe stitch with eight size 8 transparent green AB seed beads and a green leaf bead at the end.

Ingredients

green stone cabochon

fabric glue

size 8 transparent green AB seed beads

three green leaf beads

Technical Support

Supplies

Beads and Cabochons

Seed beads are the most commonly used beads in bead embroidery. They are small, rounded glass beads that come in several sizes, making them very versatile. For the projects in this book, you'll be using several sizes of seed beads: mostly 8/0, 10/0, and 11/0, and occasionally 4/0, 6/0, and 15/0. The larger the number, the smaller the bead, so size 4/0 beads are the largest beads you'll be using, and size 15/0 are the smallest. Seed beads also come in color mixes, which we can use to achieve interesting effects in the beadwork. You can purchase pre-made mixes, or make your own. You can find seed beads at bead stores, craft supply stores, and even dollar stores. I use both Japanese and Czech seed beads; note that only Czech seed beads come in size 10/0.

There is a range of quality in seed beads. The high-end Japanese seed beads are prized for the fact that their size is very consistent, and this consistency is important for many bead weaving techniques. In bead

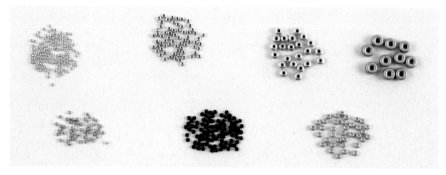

Seed beads and cylinder beads

embroidery, however, differences in size can be an asset, because when you use beads to fill a small area, it helps to have a few smaller beads to use in tight corners. So while you're working with the beads, if you come across some smaller beads, save them for such an occasion.

Seed beads come in a variety of finishes: transparent, opaque, metallic, matte, pearl, silver-lined, color-lined, Aurora Borealis (AB), fire-polish, and combinations of these.

Cylinder beads are small glass beads, like seed beads, but they are shaped like a cylinder with straight sides, and are more uniform in size and shape. We will be using size 11 cylinder beads in just a few motifs.

Crystals and other beads

You can use crystals and fire-polish beads to add some extra sparkle to your work. There are also many other bead shapes, including bugles, flowers, leaves, pearls, triangles, drops, and more. In this book you will learn how to use a variety of these bead shapes.

To make things easier, I refer to the seed bead sizes as simply 4, 6, 8, 10, 11, and 15 throughout the book.

Cabochons

Needles, thread, and other supplies

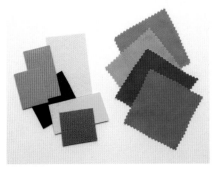

Fabric and bead backing

Cabochons are shapes made of glass, stone, or other materials. Typical cabochons have a domed shape and a flat back. Unlike beads, cabochons do not have holes to use when fastening them to fabric. Instead, we use glue, or we surround the cabochon with circles of seed beads to hold it against the surface of the fabric.

You can also use stone beads, glass beads, or flat pieces of wood painted with acrylic paint, as cabochons in your work, as long as they have a flat bottom. You can also make or buy polymer clay cabochons.

Needles, Thread, and Other Tools

The first two tools you will need are needles and thread. You need a needle small enough to go through the smallest beads. I recommend size 10 or 12 beading needles.

My thread of choice is Nymo thread, a nylon beading thread that comes in many colors. It is strong enough to handle all the components we will be using. In general, the color thread you use should match the beads you are using; if you are using several colors of beads, try using a thread in a neutral color like grey.

In a couple of motifs, we will be using traditional embroidery with embroidery floss. Floss comes in solid colors, variegated colors, and metallics.

You can use a chalk pencil and tracing paper to trace and transfer the design to your fabric. You'll also need a pair of sharp scissors and some white glue.

Surfaces

All the motifs in the book are done on solid-color fabric covering a piece of stiff bead backing, or directly on colored bead backing. These materials are suitable for jewelry like cuff bracelets, brooches, or necklaces. I also enjoy working with cotton batik fabric, which comes in beautiful colors and patterns.

I have tried several different backing materials, and my favorite is Nicole Campanella's BeadBacking. It has just the right amount of stiffness, and the needle passes through it very easily. It comes in a variety of colors, and in sizes up to 9 x 12 inches (23 x 30.5 cm).

A variety of embellishments

Techniques

Single Beads

If you are just beginning, thread your needle with about 3 ft. of thread and tie a knot at the end.

Stitching a single bead can be as simple as bringing your needle up from the back of the fabric, putting the bead through the needle onto the thread, and pushing the needle back down through the fabric on the other side of the bead. To make the stitch more secure, you can go through the bead a second time.

If the holes of a bead sit too far up from the surface of the fabric, you can add one or two seed beads on each side to hide the thread.

Embellishments

In addition to beads, there are a wide variety of other embellishments you can use in your bead embroidery. Some metal bead caps, for example, can be used as flowers. Filigree, charms, and even chandelier earring findings can find a place in a design.

Die-cut felt can add an interesting accent. You can purchase die-cut felt pieces like flowers and leaves, or cut them yourself with scissors or with a die-cutting machine that can handle felt. Look for ribbon, sequins, buttons, and trim at stores that carry sewing supplies. Scrapbooking supplies can make interesting embellishments as well. And you never know what you'll find at the dollar store!

Supplies for Individual Motifs

Each motif photo is accompanied by a diagram that you can trace onto your fabric. The diagrams specify the types of beads or embellishments used in the motifs. I encourage you to experiment with different colors and a variety of components.

Mandala Stencils

One of my favorite pastimes is drawing mandalas, and I've developed a set of stencils to make the process easier. You don't need these to stitch the motifs in the book, but they will be helpful if you want to create your own symmetrical circular designs. You'll find more information on page 126.

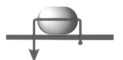

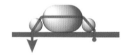

Stitching a single bead

Stitching a single bead samples

You can use this technique to stitch individual seed beads over an area of your project. This is the scatter stitch.

Scatter stitch sample

Backstitch

This is the stitch you will use most often. Use backstitch to fasten lines of seed beads to your fabric, outline a shape, or fill in an area. The line can be made up of just one type of bead or several in repeating patterns.

Push the needle from the back to the front of the fabric. Pick up two seed beads and slide them down the thread to the fabric. Then lay the beads onto the fabric, and push your needle down through the fabric at the edge of the last bead. Your two beads should be laying flat on the fabric.

Bring your needle back up at the beginning, and take the needle through the two beads. You're now ready for the next two beads. Repeat with pairs of beads until you have reached the desired length.

It is possible to use more than two beads at a time in backstitch, but using only two beads in each pass makes the beadwork stronger, and the curves smoother.

Backstitch

Backstitch samples

If you finish a line or a curve and find that the beads are not well aligned, take your needle and thread through all the beads without going through the fabric. Tug on the thread and the beads will fall into line.

Bugles are short glass tubes; they come in many colors and several lengths. Because of the way they are manufactured, the edges can be sharp and may cut your thread. So when you use these beads, place a seed bead on either side of the bugles so that your thread will not come in contact with the sharp edges.

Bugles

Bugle samples

Stacks and Fringe

The simple stack stitch is a quick and easy way to add a flat bead with a hole in the center using a small seed bead as a stop bead. First, place the flat bead where you'd like it on the fabric and bring your needle up from the back of the fabric through the center hole of the bead. Add a seed bead to your thread, and thread the needle back down through the hole in the flat bead.

In the photo, you can see examples with flower beads, metal pieces, a disc bead, and a die-cut felt flower.

You can use the same technique to add a stack of beads. Stacks like this add a lot of dimension to a beaded piece.

The same stitch can be used to create a fringe on the edge of a design.

Simple stack stitch

Simple stack stitch samples

Multiple-bead stack stitch

The bead at the top of the stack will often leave some thread showing. Because of this, I recommend using thread the same color as the top bead when stitching stacks.

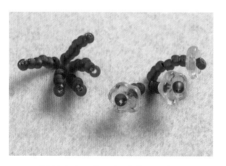

Multiple-bead stack stitch samples

Cabochon Bezel

There are several ways to create a bezel around a cabochon, and this is my favorite.

The first row of beads is stitched close around the cabochon using the backstitch. When you are getting started it will be easier if you use two alternating colors and work with an even number of beads.

Subsequent rows are worked into the beads instead of the fabric using the peyote stitch method. Bring your needle and thread through a bead, string one bead onto your thread, skip a bead in the previous row, and go through the next bead.

At the end of one round, start the next round the same way. If you have trouble visualizing this, there are several online videos that will help.

Cabochon bezel, part 1

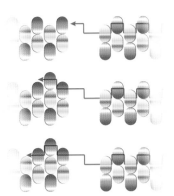

Cabochon bezel, part 2

Cabochon bezel sample, top view

Cabochon bezel sample, side view

Couching Cords and Ribbon

Couching is a technique you can use to stitch down a piece of cord. Bring your thread up on one side of the cord, and back down on the other side. You can use a thread that matches the color of the cord or a contrasting color depending on the effect you prefer.

The couching technique can also be used for long rows of seed beads. It's faster than the backstitch, but also less secure.

You can use seed bead stacks to stitch down a length of ribbon.

Loops and Picots

Loops and picots are great dimensional stitches. To create a loop, come up through the fabric, add several seed beads to your thread, and go back down through the fabric close to where you came up. If you tighten the thread, the beads will stand straight up. If you leave the thread a little loose, the loop will flop down onto the fabric. By overlapping loops, you can add great texture to your work. Also consider using shallow loops as a filler instead of backstitch.

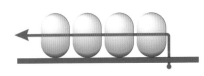

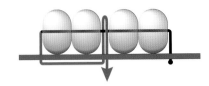

Couching

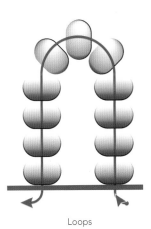

Loops

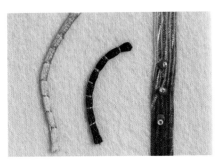

Couched cord and ribbon samples

Loops sample

A picot is a set of three beads where the middle bead stands up above the fabric. They can be used to create a dimensional line of beads that makes a nice border. If you are using two-hole buttons, a picot is a great way to hold it down.

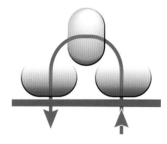

Picots

Small Leaf Stitch

This is a simple variation of backstitch, where you stitch one row of beads, for example, seven beads. Then stitch another row next to it with two fewer beads, in this example five, going through the two end beads of the first row. You can use this stitch to make small leaves in a floral design.

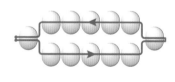

Small leaf stitch

Running Stitch and Backstitch with Thread

I like mixing some thread embroidery with bead embroidery. I use these two stitches in some of the motifs. For running stitch, simply run the needle up through the fabric from the underneath and then back down through the top of the fabric several times, making a dashed line.

Running stitch with thread

The backstitch has some similarities to the bead backstitch. In this one, you bring your needle up, then down through the fabric to make the first stitch. Then you bring the needle up where you want the next stitch to end and back down in the same spot where you went down before.

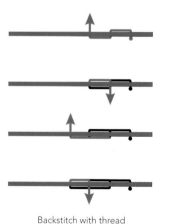

Backstitch with thread

Picots sample

Small leaf stitch sample

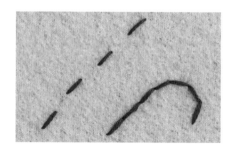

Running stitch and backstitch thread sample

Tracing and Transferring Designs

If you want to transfer designs from the book onto your fabric, you will need some tracing paper, a pen, and a chalk pencil. Put the tracing paper over the design in the book, and trace the outline with a pen.

Turn the tracing paper over, and trace the design with the chalk pencil.

Place the traced design, chalk-side down, on the fabric, and then rub lightly with your finger to transfer the chalk to the fabric.

You now have a chalk outline that you can follow to stitch the design. If the image is incomplete, you can touch it up with the chalk pencil. As long as you keep a light touch with the pencil, you will be able to brush off excess chalk.

Wood shapes and painting supplies

Painting Wood Shapes

If you want to paint wood shapes to use in your bead embroidery, here is a very simple way to paint them. I use DecoArt Dazzling Metallics acrylic paints because they are easy to use, come in great colors, and leave a beautiful shiny finish. In addition to the paint, you will need an inexpensive paint brush and some fine sandpaper.

First, if the wood piece has any varnish or other smooth finish, you need to use sandpaper to rough up the surface and give it some tooth so the paint will adhere better. Then apply a coat of paint and let it dry.

Once the paint is dry, you may find the surface is a little rough. This is because the water in the paint makes the grain of the wood rise a bit. So sand the surface, and then apply a second coat of paint. This second coat should dry to a smooth finish.

Tracing the design

Apply the design to the fabric

Add the chalk

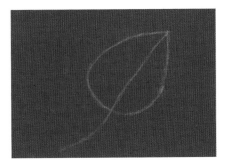

Design transferred

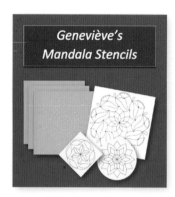

Choose a stencil

Position the stencil and mark with chalk

Using Geneviève's Mandala Stencils

Even though I designed these stencils as a drawing aid, they work great for planning a circular bead embroidery design.

There are three stencils with lines of dots at different angles; one at 10° angles, one at 15°, and one at 22.5°. Choose one based on the number of repetitions of the design you want around the circle. For example, say you want to design a snowflake motif, and you want a pattern divided into twelve sections. Twelve sections in 360 degrees means 30° per section, so choose the 15° stencil. Then transfer the dots from every other line around the circle onto your fabric as follows:

Position the stencil with the center dot in the center of your fabric, and make chalk marks through the desired holes.

You now have equally spaced points on which to place your beads so that your design will be symmetrical.

Find further information and video tutorials at: http://tangleharmony.com/shop/mandala-stencils/

Pattern transferred

Resources and Suppliers

Here are some of my favorite suppliers:

Amaryllis Creations (my mandala stencils)	amarylliscreations.com
ArtBeads (beads, embellishments, tools)	artbeads.com
Arton (beads, embellishments)	artonbeads.net
beadFX (beads, embellishments, tools)	beadfx.com
Bead Tweety (beads)	beadtweety.com
Beadwright (beadbacking)	beadwright.com
Bear With Us (wood shapes)	bearwithusinc.com
Butterfly Blue Designs (felt shapes)	etsy.com/shop/ButterflyBlueDesigns
Canada Beading Supplies (beads)	canbead.com
Fire Mountain Gems (beads, embellishments)	firemountaingems.com
Joggles (beads, embellishments)	joggles.com
Kailea (jewelry mountings)	etsy.com/shop/Kailea
Silver Dawn Jewels (charms)	silverdawnjewels.blogspot.ca
Stockade (wood shapes)	stockade.ca
That Bead Lady (beads)	thatbeadlady.com

About the Author

Following a thirty-year career in the high-tech industry, Geneviève Crabe is now devoting her time to artistic pursuits. She makes her home in St. Thomas, Ontario, Canada, where she is a teacher of bead embroidery, and the new art of Zentangle. She is working on expanding her arts and crafts business, Amaryllis Creations, by teaching and publishing. She blogs about her artistic journey and teaches online classes at CraftArtEdu.com. Geneviève is a member of Discovering Arts in Canada, the Toronto Bead Society, the St. Thomas Elgin Artists Guild, and the Canadian Embroiderers' Guild, London.

Visit www.amarylliscreations.com to find links to all of Geneviève's online homes, including her portfolio, blogs, Facebook page, Twitter feeds, and more.

Artist's Statement: *"I believe that creativity is not just the realm of a talented few, but something that all of us can learn and exercise in our lives."*

Contributors

Cindy Angiel is a multimedia artist living in Wyoming who uses creativity as a part of her pain management therapy and self expression. With more than 30 years of experience under her belt, Cindy is living proof of the healing powers that art has to offer. She explores many different art forms, but paper is the medium she enjoys the most, and she always has several pen and ink drawings in the works in her studio. Cindy is a published author who shares her drawing patterns in e-books and on her blog at the RainbowElephant.com. A strong leader in the creative community, she also runs the popular LineWeaving.com web community of repeat-pattern art enthusiasts.

Roxann Blazetich-Ozols has worked with beads for more than 10 years. At first she made finished jewelry, then began creating beaded jewelry kits (www.beadaddict.ca), which she now uses to teach beading at bead shows and stores across Canada. Recent beadwork engineering opportunities in collaboration with lampwork artists have allowed Roxann to design unique, wearable art jewelry. Her work has been featured in publications including Lark Books' *Showcase 500 Beaded Jewelry*, *Flow Magazine*, *The Glass Bead*, *A Needle Pulling Thread*, *Canadian Beading*, *Talent Next Door*, and Toronto Bead Society calendars. Roxann was a finalist in the Bead Dreams 2012 competition (Kalmbach Publishing), 1st place prize winner in the Wellington Artists Gallery 2012 exhibition, and chosen for International Society of Glass Beadmakers exhibitions in 2011 and 2012. She is a member of several bead societies and helps organize the Grand River Bead Society annual show in Guelph, Ontario.

Rose Klein is an avid beader. Embellishing fabrics and paper has been an extension of her passion for using beads in innovative ways. Recently she has been using beads and fabrics in her acrylic paintings. When she is not pursuing her craft, she and her partners are running an art gallery in Port Stanley, Ontario (www.artemporium.ca) where artists of different art mediums display and sell their work. One of Rose's beaded creations was chosen to be displayed during the 2010 Winter Olympics in Vancouver.

My name is **Denise Smeaton** and I am a beader. It always turns heads when I say that because people wonder what, or in some cases, who, I beat!! Beading is a passion, it's a hobby, and it's a collection! There is something magical about taking tiny little pieces of glass and creating something tactile, colorful, and in some cases, emotional. It's more than building, more than creating, and more than playing. A beader goes to his or her beads because of a need to express a thought, or create an idea or to follow an inspiring whisper. Inspiration comes from all around, but especially nature. Plants, flowers, trees, and moss all conspire to release the flow of creativity and make me reach for my beads! While every once in awhile, a bead may break, I really do not beat them!

Gail Smith loves beads, painting, and feeding friends and family, not necessarily in that order. She is a member of the Toronto Bead Society.

Susan Sorrell has always had a "wild imagination" growing up. Her father's job took the family all over the world, so Susan entertained herself with all kinds of arts and crafts. She didn't become serious about art until she made it her major at Winthrop University. After earning a Bachelor's degree in Visual Design, Susan worked for a short time as a graphic artist, then decided to get her Masters in Education at Converse College to teach art. Being around children was a great way to get her creative juices flowing, so she quit after 12 years and became a full-time artist. Susan calls herself a "mixed media" artist. She has been working with textiles since 1998 and hasn't tired of it yet. Combining painting, sewing, beading, and embellishing on fabric has opened new avenues to express herself. Her pieces are whimsical, colorful, and have a personal theme. Susan draws inspiration from her life and what is happening in the world. Her series of work, *Southern Fried Fiber* is inspired by her "Southern" roots. Susan lives in Greenville, South Carolina and has a studio, Little House Art Studios, located in Taylors, SC. To view more of Susan Sorrell work visit her website www.creativechick.com and www.southernpoppaintings.com.

Acknowledgments

Going back to the beginning, I want to thank Denise Smeaton for introducing me to beading and bead embroidery, and Robin Atkins for inspiration and the Bead Journal Project.

To all my contributors, thank you for sharing your creativity, with special thanks to Gail Smith, Ronit Florence, and Stephanie Dixon for generously sharing their stash.